What Others A.

Saints under Construction is an unbroken stream of redemptive truths. Beginning with regeneration, Dr. Klick compiles an assortment of topics that spiral the reader upward toward maturity in Christ; while challenging every believer to stay on the path that God has prescribed in His Word. More than random topics, Dr. Klick has skillfully woven the fabric of this work with the kinds of truths that must be understood in order to achieve consistency in Christian living. Dr. Klick is able to communicate the heart of many biblical principles by couching them in relevant stories and powerful illustrations that both sharpen the mind and pierce the heart. Always directing us to a good and sovereign God, *Saints* is sprinkled with humor and laden with compassion, hope and grace. It sets us upon a "journey of discovery" that the reader becomes increasingly eager to take. Certainly, discovering and implementing the principles in this eclectic work will speed any Christian along in the process of becoming a masterpiece of the Master's making.

Eric Burd, President of the Household of Faith Fellowship Churches.

Saints Under Construction

We are All a Masterpiece in Process

Dr. Jeffrey A. Klick

Scripture:

For we are His workmanship, created in Christ Jesus for good works, which God prepared beforehand, that we should walk in them.
Ephesians 2:10

Dedication and Thanksgiving:

To my family, both natural and by second birth, I am eternally grateful to our Lord for His placing you in my life. Thank you to my bride, our children and their spouses for the joy you bring into my world, (not to mention all those wonderful grandchildren!) Thank you Lord for Your grace and presence, and for Your continual working in my life. I love You.

A special thanks to all of you who looked over the rough draft and made it a bit less so.

Table of Contents:

Introduction:

Like most wars, the Korean War was fought over dirt and territorial boundaries. In the early 1950's, North and South Korean brothers, aided by outside super powers, exchanged bullets and death over an invisible line called the 38th Parallel. Jack Kress served in the First Marine Division on the ever-shifting front line. As we sat drinking coffee one morning about sixty years later, Jack began to talk about the war. In my thirty-eight years of knowing him, he had never done so before. "The day began like any other day," he said. "Oh, I wasn't on the front line that day, it was about 100 feet north of me," he quipped. Like many of the freezing cold days before, it was Jack's turn to take a patrol and look for snipers, mines and ambushes. As he was getting ready to begin, another solider said, "Hey Kress, let me take your place today. I need to do something this afternoon." Jack, always eager for a few more minutes of relaxation, said he could and grinned as he adjusted the rock under his head somehow trying to make it a bit more comfortable.

Sadly, and all too common to so many other days, the soldier did not survive that patrol. Estimates say that there were about 2 million men that did not come back from that war, and about 35,000 brave American soldiers were lost in the mayhem, but not Jack. He came home without a scratch. The irony was not lost on him. A chance, spur of the moment decision was the difference between life and death for Jack. Was it just chance?

Jack, along with most of the men returning from war, reintegrated into normal life. He devoted his life to weight lifting, married a lovely lady named Ruth, and together they had four children. While following each of these children's lives would be interesting, I want to focus on the second born, Leslie. Born in 1955, Leslie was born into a very hostile environment. In her world constant arguing and outbreaks of family violence were a common occurrence. Leslie learned early on that fists were useful when settling disputes and she grew into what was known in those days as a "Greaser." Fighting other girls after school and being tough was a way of life for her. A string of dysfunctional relationships with guys led to a messed up teenage young lady saturated with drinking, drugs and immorality. As her parents separated and eventually divorced, Leslie became hardened. And while she presented an image of steel on the outside, she was extremely insecure, and an emotional mess on the inside.

In 1971, Leslie was working as a busgirl at a busy cafeteria in the local mall. The employees were mostly early to mid teens that had entered into the drug culture. One young man began working there who was noticeably different. He was in his early 20's, which was old for this type of work, but in addition, he was a "Jesus Freak". For some reason strange to her, he focused on Leslie and began to share the Gospel with her. While often insulted and abused by his fellow workers, he found a listening ear with this angry, hurting girl. He encouraged her to attend a Bible Study with him and bothered her until she eventually gave in. In fact, God orchestrated a series of events to assure that her heart was ready. She began to exchange letters with a friend of her older sister who had become a Christian, and Chris often shared her personal testimony, which planted a seed in Leslie. During all this, a traumatic breakup with a dearly loved boyfriend, and the pressures of a home falling apart, all served to warm and penetrate this ice-cold heart. In November of that year, Leslie asked Jesus to be her Savior and Lord and her life would never be the same. The healing process began and she dedicated herself to following her Lord for the rest of her earthly days, no matter what would come.

Leslie left her old way of life and began a new journey. She quit dating and felt that the Lord told her to seek Him and that He would bring someone into her life when she was ready. About a year or so later a young, dirty, longhaired, smart aleck started working alongside her at the restaurant. Leslie felt strangely drawn to this skinny, smelly creature and began to share her story with him. She offered to wash his filthy clothes and they began to talk and hang out some. Eventually, this guy asked Jesus to come into his heart in July of 1973, and the two began to talk marriage. We did marry in May of 1975 and produced three children and they have produced ten children so far. Hindsight reveals that life is intriguing with all of its twists and turns.

None of us are fully aware of everything that has taken place before us that allows us to be where we are today. As Jack and I finished our coffee, I had a new glimpse of how God works. Over six decades ago, a young man made a seemingly small decision to skip patrol. Because of that one choice, he was not shot or killed. He married, had children and I married one of those children. We have had children and they have had more children. None of this would be a reality if Jack had died. We understand that this one decision was not the only one that mattered, for there have

Dr. Jeffrey A. Klick

been billions of choices by millions of people before and since Jack's that make a difference in countless lives. Our lives are intertwined in ways that are beyond comprehension, at least to our finite minds. There is an Infinite Mind and He knows all, sees all, and works all after His counsel and will, and that is mind renewing.

Often we feel our lives do not matter. We believe a lie that says we do not count for much. The truth is that what we do, or do not do, does mean a great deal and to a huge number of people, most of whom have not even been born yet. We matter and our lives have meaning and purpose because we are part of a greater plan than we can even begin to grasp.

In a moments time I was able to see some of the multitude of ramifications of a simple decision made by a teenager over sixty years ago, and I was breathless. God loved me so much that he spared Jack that day. God sent a young man, who was bullied and mocked daily to reach Jack's daughter. (Charlie Garrison, whom to this day, we cannot locate. If you know him pass this book along to him with my profound thanks!) She shared with me, we shared with our children, and literally thousands of people have been impacted. I have shared on TV and radio shows, written books, traveled to several countries, and have taught others for over 30 years. Those that have listened to or read my words have talked to many others and the story continues to unfold. The ripples from Jack's decision continue and only God knows how far they will spread.

The miracle is that I am not the only person, and Jack's decision was one of an infinite number being made by people all over the globe. Each of us makes choices every day that have long-term ramifications. Most of the results of those choices will not be revealed to us as to their impact, but rest assured, they have one. God knows them and while I cannot prove it biblically, I bet we spend some of our time with Him in the next life reviewing such things. We will worship Him as we see His complete plan unfold. We will have many moments when, like my conversation with Jack, the light turns on and we see a bigger picture. I firmly believe that understanding of this life's unanswered questions and mystery will flow into us and we will worship.

In the chapters that follow, I want to present to you a few of the foundational truths that have shaped and molded me as I have walked with the Lord. Some will be familiar and perhaps others you will not have thought much about before. I pray you will think more about them as you read this book and share whatever truth you may discover here with others.

I was invited to co-author a book on discipleship entitled, *The Discipling Church* (Trinity Press), and some of the subject matter in this book overlaps that book, so please consider reading it if you like what you read here.

As you join me in this journey of discovery, stop often and praise your Heavenly Father for His love and plans. You matter, and so does your life experience. You matter so much to God that He sent His Son Jesus to die for you. We must never forget how great a price was paid for us. Each of us has a journey and a story. What you will read in this book is some of what God has shown me along my journey, and I trust that it will inspire and challenge you in yours.

Dr. Jeffrey A. Klick

The truth is that if we are disciples of the Lord Jesus Christ, we are a masterpiece being formed by the Master Craftsman, and He does not make junk! In addition, each of us leaves footprints as we walk that will impact generations to come, if the Lord tarries. Decisions we make today might just be discussed sixty years from now over a cup of coffee.

Chapter One - Who Are We Following?

All roads do not lead to heaven, in fact, some lead to Denver.

I recently read a wise truth that stated that the Kingdom of God marches in single file behind our Lord and Savior Jesus Christ. Jesus told us that the way is broad that leads to destruction, but very narrow that leads to life. It is in fact, single file.

The issue of who we are following and serving is critical. Jesus was extremely clear:

> *No one can serve two masters, for either he will hate the one and love the other, or he will be devoted to the one and despise the other. You cannot serve God and money. Matthew 6:24*

Bob Dylan sang these lyrics a few decades ago, "You gotta serve somebody, it may be the devil or may be the Lord, but you gotta serve somebody." Sagely Bob was correct! Each of us has to settle the lordship question very early on in our walk with God. Who are we going to serve? Who is going to make the final decision? Who is sitting on the throne of our heart? The answer determines everything from how to order our days on earth to where we will spend eternity when we leave here!

Jesus, while a crowd favorite, was never a crowd pleaser. Prayerfully consider the following exchange between Jesus and the multitude that was hanging on His every word.

Now great crowds accompanied him, and he turned and said to them, "If anyone comes to me and does not hate his own father and mother and wife and children and brothers and sisters, yes, and even his own life, he cannot be my disciple. Whoever does not bear his own cross and come after me cannot be my disciple. For which of you, desiring to build a tower, does not first sit down and count the cost, whether he has enough to complete it? Otherwise, when he has laid a foundation and is not able to finish, all who see it begin to mock him, saying, 'This man began to build and was not able to finish.' Or what king, going out to encounter another king in war, will not sit down first and deliberate whether he is able with ten thousand to meet him who comes against him with twenty thousand? And if not, while the other is yet a great way off, he sends a delegation and asks for terms of peace. So therefore, any one of you who does not renounce all that he has cannot be my disciple.
Luke 14:25-33

Jesus does not pull any punches and is not attempting to win a popularity contest with these sentences. In easy to understand terms Jesus explains the cost of following Him. Love Me more than your family, yourself, and anything you may possess. Take up your cross and walk in My footsteps all the way to death. Renounce or forsake everything temporal to gain that which is eternal. If you will not do these things, you cannot be My disciple.

"Cannot" is a scary word in this context. The truth is that Jesus will not share the throne or right to rule with anyone else.

Lordship is an exclusive term and means that there is room for only one on the throne of each person's heart. It is impossible to properly serve Jesus, money, or self at the same time. Jesus demands complete abandonment of all of our life to follow Him. In our day, with an often watered downed Gospel message, this teaching does not sit well with many. We want peace, joy and happiness. We crave ease, comfort, and smooth sailing until we are rescued to spend eternity in more peace, joy, and ease. While appealing, this is not the Gospel Message.

We do a disservice to new believers when we do not explain to them the cost of discipleship. Jesus was clear to His followers, and we should be equally clear to those to whom we share the Good News. There is a high cost of following Jesus. A friend of mine said, "The gift of salvation is free; it will only cost you everything you are and ever hope to be." Jesus said to make sure you count the cost before jumping in. Have we presented the Gospel this way? Have we presented a soft Gospel or a true one?

Jesus told the rich young man in Luke 18 "to sell all he had and give it away, then come follow Me." As the young ruler left very discouraged, the disciples were given further instruction about how difficult it is for those that are rich to enter the Kingdom of God. The disciples were told that it is very hard for someone who is rich to lay their wealth down for the Kingdom. Why do they have to? Does God hate riches or something? No, Abraham, David, Solomon, and a host of other Bible characters possessed riches; however,

Dr. Jeffrey A. Klick

Lordship is exclusive, and God will not share it with money
or anyone else. If we will follow Him, He must be first and
foremost in our lives. Jesus put the challenge to this rich
young man to worship and follow Him only, and not his
money, and the call remains the same in our day. We must
serve God and use money as a tool and not get this order
mixed up.

When tested by the religious elite, Jesus explained the
principle clearly:

> But when the Pharisees heard that he had silenced
> the Sadducees, they gathered together. And one of
> them, a lawyer, asked him a question to test him.
> "Teacher, which is the great commandment in the
> Law?" And he said to him, "You shall love the Lord
> your God with all your heart and with all your soul
> and with all your mind. This is the great and first
> commandment. And a second is like it: You shall
> love your neighbor as yourself. On these two
> commandments depend all the Law and the
> Prophets." Matthew 22:34-40

There is no wiggle room in this reply! Loving with ALL of
our heart, soul and mind, includes everything we are,
dream, and think. God wants it all! When revealing
Himself to Moses, God said, "I am the Lord God, you shall
have no other god before Me." Lordship is exclusive.

Just so you know I am not overreaching or stretching
this principle too far, consider these verses and spend some
time reading the context of each one:

*Then Jesus said to him, "Be gone, Satan! For it is
written, " 'You shall worship the Lord your God and
him only shall you serve.' " Matthew 4:10*

When confronted with the temptation to short circuit
God's will, avoid the cross, and still get all the power and
glory, Jesus rebukes Satan explaining that there is only one
Lord that is to be worshipped!

*"Not everyone who says to me, 'Lord, Lord,' will
enter the kingdom of heaven, but the one who does
the will of my Father who is in heaven.
Matthew 7:21*

Lordship is not merely a word we say or give mental
assent to, but something we live out in daily obedience to
God's revealed commands. I will explain in a moment some
of what really happens to us after Jesus becomes Lord of
our life, but for now, we must understand that talking and
doing are two different things! Mouthing or giving lip
service to obedience will not suffice when standing before
our Lord; walking in His commands is what He desires.

*And Jesus said to him, "Foxes have holes, and
birds of the air have nests, but the Son of Man has
nowhere to lay his head." Another of the disciples
said to him, "Lord, let me first go and bury my
father." And Jesus said to him, "Follow me, and
leave the dead to bury their own dead."
Matthew 8:21-22*

Jesus presents a picture of following Him that includes
not living for luxury or even family connections. We must

Dr. Jeffrey A. Klick

follow Him first. Jesus is not saying that we should not take care of our families, but in comparison, we must follow Him first and fully. In Jesus' day "bury my father," was a common euphemism for "I will follow You when I am good and ready." Lordship does not work on those terms! Followers do not dictate to their Master, they obey Him.

> *Because, if you confess with your mouth that Jesus is Lord and believe in your heart that God raised him from the dead, you will be saved. Romans 10:9*

Salvation is a Lordship issue not simply a mouth confession. In the day in which Paul wrote this sentence, acknowledging any lord other than the Roman emperor was almost a certain invitation to the gladiator games, as lion dinner, not as a spectator. This confession was not a glib one.

> *Therefore God has highly exalted him and bestowed on him the name that is above every name, so that at the name of Jesus every knee should bow, in heaven and on earth and under the earth, and every tongue confess that Jesus Christ is Lord, to the glory of God the Father. Philippians 2:9-11*

Every tongue, both saved and not, will confess that Jesus is Lord. We who are born again have realized this is the future and we choose to bow now! While Jesus *is* our Savior, the term Lord is used hundreds of times in the New Testament in reference to Jesus, and Savior is used only 23 times.

*Then I saw heaven opened, and behold, a white
horse! The one sitting on it is called Faithful and
True, and in righteousness he judges and makes
war. His eyes are like a flame of fire, and on his
head are many diadems, and he has a name written
that no one knows but himself. He is clothed in a
robe dipped in blood, and the name by which he is
called is The Word of God. And the armies of
heaven, arrayed in fine linen, white and pure, were
following him on white horses. From his mouth
comes a sharp sword with which to strike down the
nations, and he will rule them with a rod of iron. He
will tread the winepress of the fury of the wrath of
God the Almighty. On his robe and on his thigh he
has a name written, King of kings and Lord of
lords. Revelation 19:11-16*

This sight is one that I only want to see from the back of
the crowd while I ride on a white horse! There will be no
doubt about Jesus' lordship on that day! Eyes of fire and
sword wielded by the King and Lord of the universe will be
a terrifying sight to those that have not bowed!

These few verses are only a small sampling of the times
Jesus is referred to as Lord. In summary, the entire
Scriptures present a uniform picture of exclusivity. One
Lord - who will it be? This is the critical decision that every
human will make. Choose wisely.

Dr. Jeffrey A. Klick

What Happens at the New Birth?

When we are presented with the Gospel we face a decision. We can accept or reject it, and many well educated people have argued for centuries over the amount of free will involved. I certainly will not solve this issue and refuse to be drawn into the discussion. I will let others attempt to clearly explain what is unknowable. What I do know, and have a glimpse of understanding, is that *after* we accept the free gift of Salvation, we are changed!

Most of us are familiar with the highly respected Pharisee named Nicodemus, who came to Jesus at night to have a private discussion. Whatever Nicodemus' reasons for coming at night, the private conversation he intended is held as the most widely known one ever. Almost everyone knows John 3:16 either from childhood, or watching sports and seeing it under an athlete's eyes, or on a big sign in the crowd. What it means is another story altogether. Before John 3:16 are these verses:

> *Jesus answered him, "Truly, truly, I say to you, unless one is born again he cannot see the kingdom of God." Nicodemus said to him, "How can a man be born when he is old? Can he enter a second time into his mother's womb and be born?" Jesus answered, "Truly, truly, I say to you, unless one is born of water and the Spirit, he cannot enter the kingdom of God. That which is born of the flesh is flesh, and that which is born of the Spirit is spirit. Do not marvel that I said to you, 'You must be born again.' The wind blows where it wishes, and you*

hear its sound, but you do not know where it comes from or where it goes. So it is with everyone who is born of the Spirit." John 3:3-8

"Born again" is a wonderful picture of what happens to us when we settle the Lordship question. Our first birth was, and is, entirely saturated with death. From our first breath we march on awaiting our last. We are born with a sin nature that stands condemned to eternal judgment with no hope of removing it. Before salvation, we are all sinners going our own way resisting God and serving our father the devil. Whether we will recognize or acknowledge this truth or not, this is the picture presented in the Scriptures.

Because of the sacrifice of Jesus on the cross for our sins, we can now, by accepting the free gift of God, be born again into a new race of people. Being born again suggests exactly what we think of when we think of being born the first time - new beginning, new heritage, new parent, new life. From the moment of new birth we are now heading to life without any death. We are new creations in Christ, all is new, the old is fading away and we look forward to what is ahead. Do not just take my word for this, consider these Scriptures:

Thus it is written, "The first man Adam became a living being"; the last Adam became a life-giving spirit. 1 Corinthians 15:45

Therefore, if anyone is in Christ, he is a new creation. The old has passed away; behold, the new has come. 2 Corinthians 5:17

Dr. Jeffrey A. Klick

For neither circumcision counts for anything, nor uncircumcision, but a new creation. Galatians 6:15

Jesus is referred to as "the last Adam" in the first verse I quoted above. The first Adam sinned and damned all of us to hell. The last Adam was a perfect atoning sacrifice and opened the way to eternal bliss with our heavenly Father. Adam is representative of the human race, and Jesus, as the last Adam is representative of a new race of people! The born-again ones - The Bride of Christ, the children of God, etc. All of these common expressions refer to the same truth that is captured in the second verse I listed above. We are new creations in Christ.

New implies that the old is gone. Everything has changed from the moment of salvation. It is almost as if we have been born again! In the final verse I listed, the raging issue of the day was how to settle the differences between Jew and Gentile. Paul clearly says that external conformity to a bunch of rules and codes does not matter, what does matter is that we are a new creation in Christ.

When we become new, everything changes. When Jesus became Lord of my life on July 25, 1973, amazing things took place. I was completely forgiven of my sins. My desires began to change instantly. Smoking, drugs, and immorality lost their grip on me. A desire for reading the Scriptures, fellowship and worship replaced them! I was a new creation and it began to show on the outside as well as inward.

I love the illustration that was shared with me years ago by a friend named Linda. Linda explained what was going on in my heart this way. Since it was so many years ago, I will have to paraphrase based on a somewhat faulty memory. She roughly said that our hearts are like a beach with boulders and rocks all over it. When we are born again, God begins to clear away the debris. First, the big boulders are removed and we quit overtly sinning. Our language cleans up, our desires for sin lessen. As the big boulders are removed the Lord begins to work on the smaller ones like un-Christ like actions and words. As we age in the Lord, He begins to sift our sand getting all the way down to attitudes. Why do we do the things we do and for whom do we do them? This can be a very long process and often painful as the Lord reveals our hearts to us. God is the one cleaning up the beach, and He will be diligent and do a complete job. Thankfully, God is also gracious in the process and does not show us everything that needs work at once.

The Lord's purpose is not to be mean, but to conform us into the image of His Son, and to prepare us for the works He has for us to accomplish while we are still on this planet. God left us here to serve Him and to share the Good News of what He has done with every one who will listen. I love this passage and it gives me great hope:

> *Beloved, we are God's children now, and what we will be has not yet appeared; but we know that when he appears we shall be like him, because we shall see him as he is. 1 John 3:2*

Because I am a new creation in Christ, I will someday be like Him! I can't wait.

Dr. Jeffrey A. Klick

It is not possible to explain everything that takes place as a result of the salvation process, but before we move on, let me share with you a few more verses to consider. First,

> *What then? Are we to sin because we are not under law but under grace? By no means! Do you not know that if you present yourselves to anyone as obedient slaves, you are slaves of the one whom you obey, either of sin, which leads to death, or of obedience, which leads to righteousness? But thanks be to God, that you who were once slaves of sin have become obedient from the heart to the standard of teaching to which you were committed, and, having been set free from sin, have become slaves of righteousness. Romans 6:15-18*

Because I am born again, a new creation in Christ, I am no longer a slave to sin. The power of sin has been defeated at the Cross of Calvary. Because of what Jesus has done, we are free. While I can still *choose* to go against God and His Word, I do not *have to* anymore by nature. I am free to serve my Lord minute by minute, and so are you if you are born again. This is indeed Good News. Before I was born again I served my flesh and sin nature and really had no choice. After salvation, I became a new creature in Christ and am now free to serve God without the strangling bondage of sin. I can still make bad choices, but I don't have to any longer.

Second, the most incredible sentence ever written and if it was not in the Scriptures I would not believe it, but because it is, I bank my eternal soul on it!

*For our sake he made him to be sin who knew no
sin, so that in him we might become the
righteousness of God. 2 Corinthians 5:21*

When I am born again I am now the righteousness of
God in Christ. Just try to get your mind around that
sentence for a bit. Jesus Christ lived the perfect, sinless life
and yet became sin for me. Many times my life has been a
wreck, yet this process of substitution takes place and now
I am perfect when viewed through Jesus' death on the cross.
If we ever get a glimpse of what this really means we will
worship freely and never complain again. This "Grand
Exchange" is beyond what I can comprehend, but I love the
Lord Jesus for it. There is an old bluegrass song which
lyrics say something about us owing a debt we cannot pay
and Jesus paying a debt He did not owe, and if it had been
written while Paul was alive, he would have been singing it
at the top of his lungs.

This brief discussion on Lordship is foundational to our
understanding of what has taken place in our life once we
are born again. We are new creations, part of a new race of
people, serving a Holy King and Lord in heaven who will
return to earth to set everything right! Our lives are no
longer our own to direct but we seek the will of our Master
and Lord. If you have not settled the lordship issue, please
do not waste another minute of your life. Every knee will
bow sooner or later, bow now and begin to live a life that
will make a difference for eternity.

There are other people who are walking in our footsteps;
where are we leading them? If we are following our Lord

Dr. Jeffrey A. Klick

Jesus, we are leading them in the right direction. If not, we need to learn another Biblical word - repent! Repentance is used often in Scripture and at its root it means, to turn around and walk in the opposite direction. By God's grace and because of Jesus' blood we can change! Prayerfully consider these two passages as we close this chapter.

> *Come now, let us reason together, says the LORD: though your sins are like scarlet, they shall be as white as snow; though they are red like crimson, they shall become like wool. Isaiah 1:18*

> *If we confess our sins, he is faithful and just to forgive us our sins and to cleanse us from all unrighteousness. 1 John 1:9*

It does not matter where we have been or what we have done, if we will confess our sins, repent and walk away from them, God will redeem our lives and use us to help others! We can experience God's forgiveness, be born again, and walk in freedom from the bondage of guilt and sin. That is a promise from the Last Adam!

In the next chapter I want to touch on another foundational topic regarding our main point of contact with God, the Scriptures. Before I do though, please pause a moment and consider these questions. I will provide some questions at the end of each chapter to help us process what has been written and to perhaps bring us closer to our Lord as we consider them.

Questions to Consider:

1. Who or what is Lord of my life? Jesus? Money? Self?

2. What does it mean to me that I have been born again and how does it impact my daily living?

3. Is there something holding me back from following my Lord with all that I am?

4. If I died today, would Jesus say, "Well done good and faithful servant," or "Depart from Me, I never knew you"? Why?

Chapter Two: Herman Who?

What we read matters greatly for it makes an imprint on our soul.

As a pastor, I have enjoyed interacting with a wide variety of people over the last thirty years or so. I also have encountered some pretty interesting methods used by people in their attempt to discover God's will. For example, some people try to discern God's will by simply closing their eyes and letting the Bible fall open. With their eyes still closed they point to a verse at random and assume that God is leading them. We probably have heard the jokes associated with this type method, for example - a person closes their eyes and opens the Bible and points and their finger lands on, "And Judas went out and hanged himself." "Oh my," says the person, "that can't be right." They repeat the process and their finger lands on, "Go ye likewise and do the same!" Still undaunted, they try one last time and their finger lands on "What you must do, do quickly." For the record, this is not the proper way to read the Scriptures! While somewhat funny, this is also sad. God, Who is the Master Communicator, has not given us His Word to make us guess as to what He wants! God is the God who speaks and Jesus is the Word of God incarnate. God does not want us to have to guess at what His will is. He sent His Son to show us, left us His Word to speak to us, and gave us the Holy Spirit to explain what He wants.

Over the years, I have also known people to take the story of Gideon and use his methods to make tough decisions. Are we to use fleeces in our day because Gideon did in his? The Apostles cast lots to make decisions, should we? How about using the example of the Patriarch's commanding their married, adult children and using that as a model for our day? Should we be selecting our children's spouses because this happened in the Old Testament, or perhaps we should only do so if we send a servant to our relatives that happen to give our camels a drink of water? Does the Scripture really promise us seventy years of life? If all of the stories in the Old Testament are given as an example for us, how should we learn from them if not by direct imitation?

One of my favorite classes in seminary dealt with the topic of learning how to study the Bible. When I first considered this topic, I thought, "Don't you just read it, and why does it matter how I read it?" Perhaps you are thinking the same thoughts. The truth is that there is a great deal of life and growth potential in simply reading the Scripture from cover to cover. I have done this myself following a reading schedule every year for about the last thirty years or so and love it.

Another truth is that we need to *understand* what we are reading and *how* to apply it, and there are some basic principles that will help us. The Bible is not like any other book ever written. In fact, it is not one book in the truest sense, but sixty-six of them. There is one theme and One main Character, but the Bible contains a great deal of variety. With many authors, multiple languages, various genres and written over a huge time span, the Bible is unique.

The Bible also claims divine inspiration, and if we read it, we will be changed. The Bible states that it is, "living, active, and able to separate soul from spirit down to thoughts and intentions of our heart." That claim is found in Hebrews 4:12 and the promise made has been proven by millions over the centuries. We must be students of God's Word, but does it really matter all that much how we read it?

Enter our friend Herman. Hermeneutics is a fancy name that basically means the science of interpretation of texts. Most of us outside of seminary will not formally run into Herman, but we should understand its basic concepts when we read the Scripture and by doing so, we learn to avoid some common errors.

I mentioned that a great deal can be gained simply from reading the Bible and that is true. In addition a great deal of weirdness, false teaching, and poor decision making can be wandered into if we do not understand some basic concepts. If we fail to realize what type of literature we are reading, to whom it was written, and how to process what we read, we can get off into some very strange teachings. By understanding some basic principles of interpretation we can avoid getting into doctrinal error and help avoid foolish decisions.

Many stories about real people are included in the Scriptures and often there is little or no commentary as to the ethics of the outcome of their actions or behavior. Judah stops and visits a prostitute and so did the two spies sent into Jericho. Later Judah is ready to kill his daughter-in-law for becoming pregnant out of wedlock, until he discovers that he is the father. Lying, stealing, immorality, and a host of activities are recorded as historical events with little comment regarding the rightness or error of the behavior.

Jacob deceived his brother, and Laban deceived him regarding both of his wives. How many wives are we suppose to have anyway? Please don't ask David or Solomon for your answer. How many years are there between verses or what century is the book geared to? Are we simply to read a story and then follow the example presented, or do we need to do some interpreting and investigating ourselves before following what we read? Excellent questions!

What Type of Literature am I Reading?

As I mentioned above, the Scriptures are actually sixty-six books and contain a wide variety of literature. We would be wise to first understand what type of literature we are reading before we begin to adjust our behavior according to the words shared. In our Scripture we will find historical narrative, poetical, prophetical, even strange picture language called apocalyptic literature and each one should be read differently than the other. Much confusion can be avoided concerning implementation, if we simply begin by recognizing what type of literature we are reading.

If I sit down to read a good novel it will be read differently than a book of poems, an instructional manual or a history lesson. Each type of literature contains a basic understanding of how it should be read. In a novel the characters are developed and the story moves from page to page quickly. In a book of poems we are to slow down and attempt to feel what the author is saying and grasp its hidden meanings. Instruction manuals are written to be followed in order, and once you figure out which one is your native language, you might actually be successful in completing the project. A history book is a recording of events that took place and many times there is little reference to whether the actions were right or wrong; they are just presented for our consumption.

These concepts are true with the Scriptures as well. What type of literature am I reading at the moment? Do I read the Gospels in the same way as I read Proverbs? How about Exodus compared to Revelation? Each was written in a particular format and style and is to be read differently. A historical narrative such as Genesis must be read and processed differently than a collection of poems like Psalms. We need to decipher what is reported as a historical fact and what is a command or principle to follow. Paul's and John's letters must be read differently than Amos' and Habakkuk's. What literature type we are reading has a direct bearing on how we read it, and what we learn from it.

After we understand what type of literature we are reading, we are ready to move on to some basic interpretation of what we are reading. We all interpret, and whatever Bible version we are reading has already gone through a major level of change from the original language from which it is taken. Our English Bibles were first written in Hebrew, Greek and some Aramaic, and have been translated into our favorite version. Many argue over which English version is the best and most faithful to the original, but regardless of which one you read, it is not the original. Someone (and usually a bunch of them) has already made many assumptions and interpretations for you. If you desire to understand the meaning of an original

Dr. Jeffrey A. Klick

word, there are many helps available to assist in this process: lexicons, Bible dictionaries, and with the advent of the internet, multiple free tools abound. The point is many scholars have already used these tools to provide you and me with a readable version of our Bible in English!

Original Intent

One early step in this process of properly reading the Scriptures is to figure out who wrote the book and who received it. In more technical terms, we are to find out what the original "hearers" of the written material would have thought about what was written, before we catapult it into our modern times. Each book we have in our Scriptures had an author and intended recipients. The book or letter was written for some purpose and we should discover what that was before we attempt to implement its contents in our modern time. Just so we are clear, none of the books were initially written to 21st Century Christians, but all of them have meaning and purpose for us!

For example, Solomon says he wrote Proverbs to increase wisdom, know instruction, and to give prudence to the simple. Joel, on the other hand, wrote to the elders and inhabitants of Israel warning them of the "Day of the Lord." We must be careful when reading Joel to understand that there are principles we can learn from this prophet, but he was writing to a specific group of people during a specific time in history. Joel's warnings have application to us, but not all of the details pertain.

In Proverbs we can read any and all of them and gain insight, wisdom and guidance from each of them. We must,

however, understand that Proverbs are true, but they are not necessarily the *entire* truth on any given subject. Neither Joel nor Proverbs was written to English speaking, high tech, Western readers originally. Joel is a prophetic condemnation to the rebellious people of God while Proverbs contains sagely sayings to help promote practical wisdom. Both are the Word of God and both contain vast amounts of truth to be gleaned. We simply need to be careful as we study these books to understand their purpose.

This is not intended to be a detailed seminary level class on the topic, so we cannot delve as deeply into this topic as we (or you) may want. However, there are many good books written that will allow you to do so if you desire! So far we have discussed learning the literature type we are reading for a proper perspective, and along with that principle, attempting to figure out the specific purpose of the book or letter written. And, to discover to whom were the contents originally intended, before we project it into our century. What it meant to the first recipients is important for our understanding and application.

Literal Interpretation

In addition to our understanding of the literature type we must also consider *how* it is to be understood. Is the passage or section we are enjoying to be taken literally or is it figurative? Most of the Scriptures should be taken at face value. There was an actual man named David who was a shepherd. This young man killed a giant, ran for his life from an insane king, and really did mess up his family after he rose to power. The same could be said for most of the characters in Scripture - they were real people, living real lives, and we are granted a glimpse into their lives.

By the way, we really are only given a small glimpse into the lives of the characters in the Scriptures. In between some verses there can be vast amounts of time and we know little of what went on during those gaps. We can make assumptions and also learn by reading some historical context type books about the century in which the people lived, but most of the time these men and women were simply going about their normal lives. We are typically given a few highlights of the lives of our Bible heroes, and very little insight into what their everyday lives looked like. Just like you and me, most of the time the folks in the Bible lived out their days in a pretty normal, boring fashion. We might see a highlight now and then, but overall we only get a glimpse of their life.

The literal interpretation should be our normal way of reading the Bible unless we are compelled to go to something else because the literal does not make any sense. There are parts of the book of Daniel and Revelation that simply must not be literal but figurative, or at least not literal from our human understanding. There are beasts, dreams and scenes that seem more in line with a science fiction movie than the Scriptures. We must learn to read these passages with something other than the typical literal mindset. Eating scrolls, angels standing on oceans, wheels within wheels, etc. are all images that we can't really say we have even seen!

Malcolm, a man you will meet a bit later in this book, had a wonderful illustration for these types of issues. When

Malcolm would travel to the bush country in Africa, he would discuss matters with the natives that they simply had no way of understanding. These natives had lived their entire lives without TV or any contact with the outside world. Attempting to explain to these men what a fifty story high rise apartment building looked like was a chore. About as close as Malcolm could get was to say it was like fifty huts on top of one another. The natives sort of received a mental image, but not quite the same as a drive in New York or Hong Kong would have accomplished. The same can be true of the Apostle John's Revelation. John is using earthly language to explain heavenly pictures. We sort of get it, but we will really understand when we walk down the streets of gold! Some day we will understand all, for now, we know in part. So, when we encounter passages that must be taken in a way other than literal, we need to be careful in being adamant about their interpretation. I like to say, "Just because you are adamant does not mean you are correct; you might just be adamantly wrong."

Scripture Interprets Scripture

Another necessary principle is to understand that the Scriptures are without error in the original manuscripts. Being errorless, the Scriptures become our standard of a moral value system and a measuring rod of our behavior. If there seems to be a contradiction, which there is none, the issue most likely resides in our failure to understand the context or other Scriptures that shed light on the verse in question. This leads to the principle of "Scripture interprets Scripture."

Dr. Jeffrey A. Klick

This principle means that no part of Scripture will contradict another part of itself. And, by extension, if we are attempting to create a doctrine or behavioral pattern that seems to be approved by one section of Scripture, but forbidden in another, we must not go forward with our behavior. The Pharisees were masters at ignoring this principle. Consider Jesus' confrontation around the subject of helping parents:

> *Then Pharisees and scribes came to Jesus from Jerusalem and said, "Why do your disciples break the tradition of the elders? For they do not wash their hands when they eat." He answered them, "And why do you break the commandment of God for the sake of your tradition? For God commanded, 'Honor your father and your mother,' and, 'Whoever reviles father or mother must surely die.' But you say, 'If anyone tells his father or his mother, "What you would have gained from me is given to God," he need not honor his father.' So for the sake of your tradition you have made void the word of God. You hypocrites! Well did Isaiah prophesy of you, when he said: "'This people honors me with their lips, but their heart is far from me; in vain do they worship me, teaching as doctrines the commandments of men.'"*
> *Matthew 15:1-9*

The religious rulers had taken one part of Scripture and ignored another and Jesus rebuked them for it. There is nothing inherently wrong with setting aside money for God's work, but there is something wrong when we violate God's commands to do so as did the Pharisees. All of Scripture provides a context for all of Scripture!

If we are considering a behavior or life choice that clearly contradicts any part of Scripture we are in error. God revealed Himself in greater and greater detail as the Scriptures unfolds, and we also gain further insight into more of what He expects from His children. The ultimate revelation of God is in Jesus Christ, His Son. In the famous Sermon on the Mount, Jesus repeatedly said, "You have heard it said, but I say," thus equating Himself with God, the author of the Scriptures. As Jesus furthered clarified what was intended by commands given by His Father to Moses, He shook the religious community to the core!

Scripture does not contradict itself regardless of what some people boldly declare. If someone says that to you, ask them to give you one, two or five examples. They most likely are parroting someone else's viewpoint and probably have not even read the Scriptures. For our purposes, we need to understand that ultimately Scripture does the best job of interpreting itself for us.

No verse stands alone and each one has a context that includes the verses around it, the paragraph, the chapter, its own book, and the entire Bible! We must resist taking one isolated verse and building a doctrine with it. If it is an important doctrine, this teaching or principle will appear in multiple places and be clarified and strengthened by other verses. There is limited space in the Scriptures and the Holy Spirit was diligent to make sure that what was important was repeated! As an example, consider how many times we are told to love one another versus the complete lack of instruction on how to conduct a church service.

Dr. Jeffrey A. Klick

The Scriptures touch on many topics and some are covered in greater detail than others. Before making an ironclad doctrine, make sure the topic you are exploring is covered in many places. Establishing a doctrine on one isolated passage is dangerous and typically ends up being divisive. Let us be very clear on the teachings that the Scriptures repeat and let us hold more lightly the teachings that are not repeated. Many good people of faith disagree over passages of Scripture and we must learn how to walk in love toward those who don't quite see everything the way we do.

The Old Covenant is Filtered through the New Covenant

The Holy Book we study is broken into two main sections typically referred to as the Old and New Testaments. The word "testament" could also be translated covenant, and I really prefer that word picture. The story from Genesis to Revelation is the unveiling of God to His creation and what He did to accomplish redemption. In the Old Covenant God dealt with His people that came from Abraham. Almost everything recorded for us is pointing us toward, and moving us along to the birth of Christ. In the New Covenant we have the full revelation of God to His creation in the Person of Christ. After the Gospels we have the history of the Church and everything either points back to Christ or to His return! Bottom line - it is all about Jesus from cover to cover! As we read the Old Covenant we must understand that it has to be filtered and interpreted through the New Covenant. Hebrews states it this way:

But as it is, Christ has obtained a ministry that is as much more excellent than the old as the covenant he mediates is better, since it is enacted on better promises. For if that first covenant had been faultless, there would have been no occasion to look for a second. Hebrews 8:6-7

The Book of Hebrews explains that Jesus is better than Moses, angels, and anything Old Testament. Jesus is the new High Priest and has instituted a brand new covenant with God's people. The New Covenant was promised through the prophetic writings of Jeremiah and quoted here in Hebrews:

For he finds fault with them when he says: "Behold, the days are coming, declares the Lord, when I will establish a new covenant with the house of Israel and with the house of Judah, not like the covenant that I made with their fathers on the day when I took them by the hand to bring them out of the land of Egypt. For they did not continue in my covenant, and so I showed no concern for them, declares the Lord. For this is the covenant that I will make with the house of Israel after those days, declares the Lord: I will put my laws into their minds, and write them on their hearts, and I will be their God, and they shall be my people. And they shall not teach, each one his neighbor and each one his brother, saying, 'Know the Lord,' for they shall all know me, from the least of them to the greatest. For I will be merciful toward their iniquities, and I will remember their sins no more." In speaking of a new covenant, he makes the first one obsolete. And what is becoming obsolete and growing old is ready to vanish away. Hebrews 8:8-13

God's plan from the beginning was to have a personal relationship with His creation and Jesus made that possible. If you read the entire book of Hebrews you will gain a picture that is clear; the Old has been replaced with the New. Jesus is now the mediator of a new and better covenant, cut in His own blood.

What this means regarding how we read and interpret the Scriptures is that we must filter everything in the Old Testament through the more complete New Testament. Jesus did this quite often when He addressed food issues, Sabbath and holy days, the Law of Moses, Psalms, and other Old Testament Scripture. Jesus explained that many of these shadows were fulfilled in Him.

As we read the Old Covenant, and we should, we must realize that there is a new and better covenant now. We are not to go back under the Old for God has replaced it with the New. Better promises, a new High Priest, and no longer a shadow, but the real thing, and that is Jesus! God now views His people, not through the Law, but through the finished work of Christ! We are now the Bride of Christ, the children of the King, and heirs with Christ. When we read the Old Covenant we must never forget this.

When we read the Old Testament prophets for example, most of them were speaking to a hard, calloused, rebellious people, not the Bride of Christ. To transport judgments and promises of destruction into the New out of the Old is a potential mistake. We also must filter each promise we find in the Old through the lens of the New. When God said something to Israel for example, was it a perpetual promise or did it have a time limit that expired when Jesus came? A great deal of confusion can result if we mix up our Covenants! The Law was never intended to do what only Jesus could do. The Law did not offer complete forgiveness of sins, only a temporary cover, and most of the time condemnation. Complete forgiveness is only possible through the shed blood of Jesus Christ.

When we consider a command, law, promise, or anything that we wonder about in the Old Covenant, we should seek out what the New Covenant stated about it to clarify and deepen our understanding. Did Jesus or one of the other writers in the New Covenant discuss this topic? If we read all of the food laws in the book of Leviticus for example and wonder if they apply to us, what should we do? Jesus clarified and settled this issue in Mark 7 and Mark even made sure we didn't miss it with his note in parentheses on verse 19: (Thus he declared all foods clean.) The New gives further insight into the Old. We are to be students of the entire Word of God, and as we are, we gain a deeper insight into God's glory and purposes.

Herman Summary:

All of us have someone in our life that will eventually look to us for wisdom and perhaps clarity regarding a personal situation. We will at that time draw on God's grace, the Holy Spirit, and the written Word of God for our answers. We need to be students of the Bible who know

Dr. Jeffrey A. Klick

how to "rightly divide" the Word of God. Our spouse, children, work associates, and others will be impacted to some degree by how we process the Scriptures and what we share with them. We want to be as accurate as possible to make sure we are helping as much as possible.

When we pick up the Bible to read, we should consider what type of literature we are reading and to whom it was written. Next, we consider if what we are reading is meant for all people at all time, or for a specific few. If what we are reading is directive, for example, are there other verses that confirm or reinforce what we believe it is saying. If we are in the Old Testament, is there anything that further explains what we are reading in the New Testament? While there is a great deal more we could do, we certainly should not do less! We are students of the Word of God and we want to be good ones.

So, let me close this chapter with some thoughts as to why all of this is so very important. We have been given the Word of God, and as believers we love to read, study, and attempt to shape our daily lives by it. Beyond that, we attempt to learn what God has desired to communicate to us through His Word and obey it in order to please Him. Because we honor God's Word, we want to do everything we can to make sure we are reading it in such a way as to understand it clearly, and share the truth of it accurately.

The Holy Spirit was given to us and part of the reason was to bring to our minds understanding of God's Word. We should fill our minds with Scripture so the Holy Spirit has plenty of material to use in our daily lives! The Holy Spirit was also given to reveal Christ, and He is to be found on every page of the Scriptures!

Please consider the following questions before moving on into some thoughts as to why we remain on earth after salvation.

Questions to Consider:

1. What am I filling my mind with, the Scriptures or something less?

2. Am I reading the Scriptures in a fashion that will lead me into truth or error?

3. Do I understand the principles explained in this chapter? Are they really that important?

Chapter Three: Created to Interact

We were made for relationships even though they often hurt.

Many years ago, I used an illustration to explain how our lives interact with each other and it still is applicable for us today. *Bumper Car Theology* was the term I coined and on the pages that follow I want to share a bit on the topic of "crashing" into each other! We were created to impact those around us and the picture of a bumper car might be helpful in explaining why.

I have always loved carnivals and amusement parks. The lights, noise, and crowds cause the blood to flow and the pulse to quicken. The smell of popcorn and cotton candy, and the sound of children laughing with excitement brings joy to my heart and a smile to my face.

With all of these sights and sounds, there is one ride that captured my heart years ago. I love the ride above all the others combined. It is not the newest or most exciting ride. Usually the ride is old and rickety and many times it is broken down. You cannot ride it if you are pregnant or have back or neck problems. While I never been pregnant, I do have both neck and back problems, but I still ride as often as I can.

Maybe it is the concept of being totally reckless that attracts me so much, or the fact that I can crash into someone and not be sued that draws me to this ride. The whole purpose of the ride is to crash into as many people possible in the shortest time available. The point is not to go fast but to smash into everyone within sight, hitting everyone in the front, back or side as hard and as often as you can.

It could be that it is my secret wish that I could drive my car like this on the highway that compels me to strap myself into the small, metal car. Those little hunks of tin tied to the ceiling with a metal band to provide power to the slow moving tanks are a wonderful invention. The ride was probably invented by a bunch of chiropractors, but I love this amusement. The ride is, of course, bumper cars.

As I have pondered life's journey it seems to me that much of our existence is similar to a giant bumper car ride. Every morning, we awake and no sooner are our feet on the floor than we begin to "crash" into someone. Our spouse, our children, or even our family pet is in our sights to bump. When we walk out the door we get into our cars and behold, many are around that we can "ram," not literally of course, but the urge is there sometimes as I drive down the highway!

What really happens in bumper cars? Two objects "bump" into each other and both are changed. Sometimes there is a major change in direction and other times simply a tiny redirection of the previous course. No matter how small, each and every time there is a change.

What happens when two individuals come in contact with each other as we walk through our days? Both are changed in some way, occasionally in a major way and sometimes a subtle way, but both are changed. Perhaps it is change for the better or maybe not, but change always takes place. Like the bumper cars that collide, a change of direction happens with each and every contact. We spend our whole life "bumping" into others, and as a result, we are always changing direction, both theirs and ours. The Scripture puts it this way:

"Iron sharpens iron, and one man sharpens another." Proverbs 27:17

When two pieces of iron clang sharply, both are changed because sparks fly and the metal is forever altered by the contact. No matter how small or insignificant the change may seem, the iron is changed. The same is true in bumper cars and the same is true in personal relationships. We bump into folks every day and both are changed as a result of the contact. Think of how many bumps are happening in the world of social media? Millions of tweets, FaceBook comments, and blogs are exchanged minute by minute, and each one leaves a mark of some sort!

The question to consider is, "how are those I interact with changed?" Are people being changed for better or for worse as a result of our contact? Change always happens, but rarely do we know which direction we are knocking people. God sometimes allows us to see the results of our actions, but most of the time we are not even aware of what our "bump" has accomplished.

Many of us question our existence sooner or later. "Why am I here?" or "Am I just wasting my life?" or "The world would be better off if I was gone," or countless other versions of this thinking are entertained by us humans. We have a tremendous need to feel like our life has meaning

Dr. Jeffrey A. Klick

and value. We all want to make a difference in our world and I have struggled with this battle my entire ministerial life. While outsiders would look at my ministry and say it was successful, I would struggle weekly with the same question: "Am I doing anything of value?" Often on Monday morning, I would blow the dust off of my résumé and consider doing anything other than being a pastor. Most men and women I know struggle with the same concerns regardless of vocation. We need to believe that our life matters.

Part of the answer for me is to understand that my life is supposed to come into contact with people and that God is superintending each event to further His work. My life is a series of bumping into people and redirecting the course of both of our lives. Each encounter has an impact of some sort. Each conversation, each confrontation, each counseling session, each sermon, and even each phone call, has an impact. I may never see the results of our collision, but God does. God, and God alone, is the only One who can properly evaluate the worth, success, and true measure of a lifetime of bumping. I may never see the "fruit" of my bumping, but I will keep on bumping. It cannot be avoided. Unless you live on a deserted island, you will have contact with others. Each decision we make carries ramifications for others. What a thought, and if it were not for the grace of God everyone would probably live alone in a cave! God does not want us to live alone and therefore we must learn how to live with others.

Whose responsibility is it to make sure I really do have an impact in someone's life? Maybe a better way to say that is, how do I know I will do something, anything, which has value? The answer is God of course. The Scripture on the opening page of this book is:

> *"For we are His workmanship, created in Christ Jesus for good works, which God prepared beforehand, that we should walk in them"*
> *Ephesians 2:10*

This is one of my "life" verses and has kept me on course many times when I simply wanted to quit. I am God's workmanship. I am a masterpiece in process. Of course, the emphasis is on the "in process" part. However, each and every one of God's children is a masterpiece in progress. God is the master craftsman who never makes junk or mistakes, only masterpieces. Each one of God's children was created with a purpose. This understanding of process is also why it is so important to not judge one another. We simply do not know what the Master is currently working on in His masterpiece's life. Only He does. What I think God should be working on in someone else's life is very limited by my human understanding. God knows the entire process from beginning to end. God knows exactly what He is working on as He is working, and the truth is, He is the only one Who does!

Do you see that purpose of being God's workmanship? "For good works." You and I were created to do good works. I am not saved by good works, but once I am saved I will do them. We were created by God, in Christ Jesus, to do good works. God's plan is for us to do good works that

Dr. Jeffrey A. Klick

He has prepared for us to do. So, whose responsibility *is it* to make sure my life has value? God is the one who is working on this masterpiece called "Jeff." God is the one who has a plan and a purpose and He will see that I accomplish it, because God cannot fail.

The problem comes in with *our* view of God's work. I want to see the results of my labors and the fruit of what I have done. But, I am growing to realize that only God has the complete view of my life to evaluate properly the fruit of it. Only the Master Craftsman knows the process needed to achieve the finished product, and what I should ultimately look like. Anyone looking over the shoulder of a master craftsman has no idea what is going on in the mind of the artist. It is easy to second guess and even criticize the work going on, but we simply do not see the finished product as the Master does.

Michelangelo created one of the most famous statues ever made from a piece of marble that others had declared as worthless junk. The statue of David is still on display and millions view it every year. Only Michelangelo saw the potential in that hunk of marble and only God can see what is in the hunk of flesh known as man. God specializes in using broken people and those considered worthless for His glory! We give up too soon, but God does not make junk, only masterpieces.

All of my life I have been bumping into other masterpieces that are also works in progress. As we make contact with others, we are formed and shaped by the Master's hand. Some are dented, chipped, or realigned, while others are barely scratched or we hardly noticed the contact, but the Master is always at work. Irritations, conflicts, heartbreaks, and countless other collisions all mold and shape us into what the Master desires. Teachable moments, conversations, prayers, and sermons all move us along the path God has for us. God is always at work and has a master plan for each one of us. Sometimes we may catch a glimpse of what He is doing, but most times, we simply call it daily life.

Bumping into God

Our bumper car ride really begins with God in front of us. Until we bump into Him, our life has no purpose or meaning. Until we submit to Jesus as Lord, we will wander through a meaningless existence and not realize any eternal good. Without a life-giving encounter with God, we have nothing of value to give or share with anyone. We can only take from each one we meet, stealing what we can from people, and leaving them less than they were before we met them. But, once we bump into God we are forever changed! After we are born again we now have Life living inside of us. Bumping into God is unlike bumping into any other person. God does not move or change and is completely unaffected by our crash into Him.

"Everyone who falls on that stone will be broken to pieces, and when it falls on anyone, it will crush him..." Luke 20:18

Dr. Jeffrey A. Klick

However, when we bump into God, we are broken, and if we resist Him we will be crushed. God cannot be pushed, moved, or changed by anything anyone does. Unlike humans, God will not be moved, and since He is already perfect, there is no need for growth or change.

So, before we have anything of value to offer anyone else, we must come to the unmovable One. We must fall on the Rock and be broken. We confess our sins, ask for forgiveness and accept Christ's blood as our atonement. Once we have been saved, born again, given new life, redeemed, and set free, then we have something to offer all those people we will soon be bumping into. If we desire to make a lasting impact we must first be broken by the Rock that will not move. We humble ourselves before our God and repent of our pride and sins. Even though we will still take from others as we bump into them, we now have something of value to give them. We are containers of Life and we can leave deposits everywhere we go. We receive His forgiveness and empowerment, and then we are ready to begin this adventure called the Christian walk, or as I am looking at it, bumper car crashing.

Bumping into God simply begins this process of change. After our encounter with Him, then we begin to see all our other crashing partners in life with different eyes.

Bumping into Your Spouse

Marriage is supposed to be an example of the relationship between Christ and the Church, as stated in Ephesians 5:32, which is a love affair that will last for all eternity with the husband (Christ) loving and laying down His life for His Bride (the Church). It would not be much of a stretch to say that many Christian marriages fall short of this goal. Some are simply war zones with occasional truces, and others end in divorce with around the same ratio as the non-Christian world. Somewhere the Church has failed to walk the Christian talk in the home.

From the beginning God had a plan for marriage. Simply put, God knew that it would take two people to adequately represent Him to the world of unbelievers. Both male and female would be necessary to properly reflect the character of God. When God created Adam in the garden He looked and said, "This is pretty good, but he still needs something. He needs a woman to be complete." Well, what He actually said was:

> "...It is not good that the man should be alone; I will make him a helper fit for him." Genesis 2:18

This passage has interested me since I became a Christian. Adam had everything a human could want. He was in perfect fellowship with God. He had no sin to cloud his judgment or reasoning. He wouldn't age, die of any disease, and basically had a perfect situation. But, God said he needed a helper. Now, "helper" can mean a couple of things. First, helper can mean that this person is sent to wait on, serve, and take care of my needs, similar to a servant or slave. Or second, helper can mean someone to come along side and help bring to completion. I believe the latter idea is what God had in mind. Adam had no needs before Eve was created. He didn't need his house cleaned or laundry done. Meals were already provided and Adam had God to talk with, so conversation was not an issue.

So why the need to create Eve? Adam was incomplete without her. From the very beginning God desired for the married couple to become one. It would take both to accurately represent the nature and character of God. Both would be necessary to train the children and be a representation of Christ and the Church to the world. Even in Adam's perfect situation God knew he needed a helper in order for him to become what God desired. Thus marriage was born, mates were given, and the crashing began!

Shortly after you are married, say three minutes or so, the realization that you are vastly different than your spouse hits - not only physically, but emotionally, mentally, and spiritually. The opportunities for bumping into each other are unlimited. Crashes of all sizes and shapes happen daily. The process of two becoming one takes a lifetime and is not a calm process. Both people will be challenged to die to themselves daily. An illustration to help picture this is river rapids. As two streams merge into a river the water is often tumultuous. But, downstream the river is deeper and stronger that either of the two streams. In marriage, the initial coming together as husband and wife often is the roughest water, but later on the river runs deep and smooth.

Most marriages are a super highway of opportunity for crashes, and I believe God planned it this way from the very beginning. I have often said, "If two people are identical, one of them is not really necessary." If God wanted two "Adams" He would have created them. He did not. He created an Eve and she was vastly different than Adam, and wives today are still vastly different than husbands. They think differently, react differently, and have different needs than their husbands. So conflict is inevitable and I believe part of God's plan.

God desires for men to learn to lay down their lives for their wives and for wives to learn to respect and honor their husbands (See Ephesians 5:22-32.) The key word in that sentence is "learn." It is a process and will take the better part of a lifetime to get good at it. God knew exactly what each and every one of us needed to help us become what He wanted.

Once you are married you are now married to the correct spouse, and there is no need to go looking elsewhere. God will use our choices and make something good from them even if we make bad ones. Within your own marriage God has provided ample opportunities for growth and bumping into each other. With each collision we have the chance to grow and become more Christlike. Almost every day you will be given the chance to become more like Jesus. A word will be said, or an activity will take place that will rub us the wrong way. What do we do with these irritations? What do we do with all those crashes going on in our marriages? It seems like no matter which way I turn I get hit again. I would suggest that we learn from them and use them to drive us to the cross of Christ. Every time we have a crash we are given an opportunity to grow. Each irritation and disappointment is another growing experience. As we learn to die to ourselves and

Dr. Jeffrey A. Klick

embrace the cross of Christ we will grow in being more Christlike.

Another reason God provided marriage is to make sure we have ample opportunity to crash into someone *and* be instruments of change for good. It is impossible to repeatedly crash into someone without change happening. We must make sure we are bumping towards the goal of godliness and spiritual gain. Often we want to ram our bumper car into our spouse to hurt them because we are hurt and we want them to feel our pain. This is rarely constructive and often causes major injuries. The goal of bumping each other is to move us along the right path towards Christ and His will. As we bump into each other through discussions, conflicts, emotional crises, and stressful times, we are changed. God wants us to be purposeful in our crashing and not vindictive. Love must be our motivation, and revenge is not part of love.

What if only one spouse wants to crash for the good? Go ahead and ram away…remember both cars are moved in every crash. Just make sure you are ramming for Jesus and not for the Devil! We have to be constantly examining our motives of why we do the things we do and what are we trying to accomplish. God has ordained that each married couple will have many situations where they think, act, and react differently. This is not because God was bored and desired some entertainment, but because He wanted the couples to bump into each other and grow together. Each one of these potential crashes gives opportunity for change to happen to both spouses. I also believe God allows both spouses to grow at different rates so there will be even more times of bumping. God knows that each person needs others to help keep them on the course. What better way to assure a life of bumping than marriage?

If you have a longing to know that you are making an impact, you do not have to look any further than your own marriage. This relationship is full of potential for impact if we ask God for the eyes to see. The fruit of embracing the differences in our spouse will be great if we can ever get over the differences in the first place. God gave you exactly what He knew you *needed* to become what He wants you to become – a mature man or woman of God with a sanctified bumper car. Learn to embrace the differences instead of resisting them. We all need to realize that God has given us our spouses to help us move to maturity, not to torture us. One way to look at our progress is to ask these questions – "Is my spouse better or worse as a result of our marriage?" "After 5, 10 or even 30 years of marriage is my spouse more or less Christ-like as a result of my bumping into him or her?" Our God is a God of hope so don't get discouraged with your answer to those questions. Regardless of how you have done up to this point, God can change everything if we will simply humble ourselves and allow Him!

When Christian marriages begin to reflect Christ, the lost and dying world will take notice. Godly men that learn to love their wives, as Christ loved the church, and laid down His life for her, will stand out in a crowd. Christian women that respect, honor and support their husbands will be vastly different than the "normal" wife of today. I pray that our marriages will grow to the place where we really are being an example of the love between Christ and His

Dr. Jeffrey A. Klick

Bride. This type of love is rare in our dark world, and as we shine before the darkness, the light will break through.

Bumping into Your Children

Another significant tool that God provides for us to become all He intends, are children. In most homes, the blessing of offspring soon arrives and then the potential for ramming is magnified exponentially! I will cover this a bit more in a later chapter but for now consider these Scriptures.

> *"Sons are a heritage from the LORD, children a reward from him. Like arrows in the hands of a warrior are sons born in one's youth. Blessed is the man whose quiver is full of them. They will not be put to shame when they contend with their enemies in the gate." Psalms 127:3-5 (NIV)*

Children are indeed a rich blessing and if we do a good job of raising them, we will be qualified to speak with authority. We will be able to say like the apostle John

> *"I have no greater joy than to hear that my children are walking in the truth." 3 John 1:4 (NIV)*

The inverse is true also – no greater heartache has a parent than to know that their child is walking in lies and errors. In more than three decades of interaction with parents I find this to be a heartbreaking reality. Rebellious teens and adult children are the major source of tears of grief to their parents. There is no joy when we see our children cast off our faith and walk the way of the world. Children that are a rich blessing and joy comes with a significant cost to ourselves. The price tag includes investing whatever time and energy is necessary to see our children walk with God. While it is ultimately God who draws our children to Himself, we as parents are charged with leading them daily by our words, actions and life example.

No matter if you have a large quiver or economy size; these "arrows" can help you grow into Christ-like maturity. The stress and pressure of raising a family should "bump" us towards Christ. If we take the task as seriously as God does, we will soon realize how dismal of a job we are doing. Shaping and molding a young person is a full-time job. We as parents are "god in the flesh" to our children, and most of us realize that we are not anything like God!

God allows us to have children so He can work His will into our lives. We as parents are given the task to raise these children to the glory of God. Much bumping will soon take place in the average home. Soon after the little bundle of joy is brought home, it is apparent that life will never be the same. Crying, feeding and changing diapers are just the beginning of the process. Issues like less sleep, hours of talking, corrections, disciplining, more talking, and more prayer than you ever imagined go into rearing children. As the little will of the new child begins to come into focus, the bumping process will burst into full bloom. Growth opportunities will abound for all involved!

Dr. Jeffrey A. Klick

Often children can bring out the best or worst in parents. My main point here is that God will use children to mold and shape the parents as they struggle with molding and shaping the children. Many people can relate to the sentence: "I never knew I had a temper before I had children." As we struggle with the process of child training, we will see many areas in our own life that needs correction. Our relationship with our spouse changes, and again, there are ample "bumpings" that will take place. Discussions over discipline methods, interpretations over degrees of rebellion and rejection of parental authority, types of schooling, and a host of other areas, all provide for more growth opportunities in the marriage.

One issue that becomes apparent is that parents generally focus on what is wrong rather that what is right with a child. We want our children to be better than we were. We don't want them to have to make the same mistakes we have made so we try to guide them around our weaknesses. Parents often can see their own faults very clearly in their children and are driven to help root it out. We tend to focus on the 10% wrong we see and rarely focus on the 90% right. This drives many children to almost a hopeless situation of never being able to please their parents. God does give parents insight into their children, not to beat them down, but to help them overcome their flaws. Someone said that a good rule of thumb is ten parts praise to one part correction, and that may even be low.

God gives us our children to help us because He loves us. The Scripture is clear that children are a blessing not a curse. Part of that blessing is the change that comes into everyone's life as a result of the children being born. Daily opportunities to grow and be more conformed into the image of Christ result from that blessing. It really doesn't matter if we have one child or a dozen, the crashing will go on daily. Multiple children simply expand the possibility of crashing more often! Children crashing into other children, husbands and wives bumping into each other, and the parents always running into or being run into by their children, makes the family a great place to grow!

Learning to look at our spouse and children as opportunities to become more Christlike will help our attitudes as difficult times arise. In every family there are times of struggle, failure and heartache. If we were or could be perfect, we would not need to throw ourselves upon Christ; we would not need prayer or the power of the Holy Spirit. Every person is different and so is every family. God's desire is to receive as much glory as possible from every one of His children and their actions. Expect trials, difficulties, and yes, even failure as part of the journey.

When we fall, we fall on the Rock and we will be restored. If we invest wisely in our families, we have a greater potential to reap a reward of joy and a life-long relationship than if we do not even try. As our children grow the challenges change, but they never go away. Diapers and curfews fade, and marriages and grandchildren arrive, and we as parents have even more folks to bump into! Our prayer life should increase as our family ages, expands, and leaves home, not decrease. Adult children provide a whole new arena for bumping and we will spend

Dr. Jeffrey A. Klick

the rest of our lives crashing into each other, hopefully we will crash for the good and push each other towards Christ.

Bumping into Friends and Work Associates

If we ever venture outside of our homes, we will probably meet other people. If we meet them more than a few times they often become friends. Friends provide yet another opportunity for growth. If you spend much time with anyone you will soon have plenty of ramming situations. An older preacher told me one time, "Wherever two or three gather, an argument will soon arise." That of course, is a play off of what Jesus had said about two or three being together and He would be there with them. It is inevitable that disagreements and irritations will arise when people interact. God makes sure that something *will* happen to allow for a misunderstanding to take place. Why? God wants us to mature and grow up. Hurt feelings, insensitive words, misread looks, and many other situations, allow for us to "sharpen" each other, or as I would say, bump into each other. I will cover the arena of forgiveness and bitterness in a bit more detail in a later chapter so I won't develop it here, but they are both critical concepts to understand.

Which way will we push each other when the bumping occurs? Will we push each other towards Christ or some other direction? Since it is simply impossible for two people to spend much time together and there not be some type of disagreement, how should we look at those disagreements? Each and every one of these situations is God-given to help us become more like Him.

The Lord wants us to be able to love people and disagree with them in an agreeable fashion. The possibilities are unlimited for arguments. Politics, religion, family, extended family, sports, holidays, traffic, and cookouts. You name it and folks have argued over it and ended friendships because the other one would not agree with them.

Friends should be those that are helping us to grow and mature in Christ. Problems will arise, but we should be able to bump into each other and not get out of our cars and beat each other up!

"Faithful are the wounds of a friend, but deceitful are the kisses of an enemy." Proverbs 27:6 (NASB)

A true friend should be able to speak into our life and point out blind spots. Blind spots are those things we do not see but are often clear to others. If we refuse to receive correction from our friends, then our enemies will certainly point them out to us, but not from the same motivation. True friends love us and want us to succeed and are therefore willing to endure our potential negative reactions to their pointing out of our faults.

"A man of too many friends comes to ruin, but there is a friend who sticks closer than a brother." Proverbs 18:24 (NASB)

Dr. Jeffrey A. Klick

Most people will have a limited number of friends that stick with them through their life, and according to this proverb, that is not a bad thing. As we grow and perhaps get married, then have children, our set of friends often changes. We tend to want to be around those of like interest. I have often asked for a show of hands when I speak to a crowd on this topic. I will ask, "How many of you have a group of friends that you were close to in high school? You know, people that you did something with all the time and promised to always be friends." In crowds from 200-3,500 almost every hand goes up. Then I follow up the question with this one: "How many of you are still running with the same crowd today?" Almost no hands go up. Why? Because friends come and go. People move on, change locations, get married, or get fed up with each other. Most of us can only handle a few close friends in our lives at any given time or for any length of time!

God will often give these people insight into our lives to help us grow. Their "wounds" can be something that produces life in us, or is allowed to ruin us. It all depends on how we react to their "ramming" into us.

In addition to friends, many of us will work at some type of employment in our lives. These co-workers will be flawed folks just like us, and soon crashes will begin. Office politics, miswritten emails, gruff bosses, rude partners, stressful deadlines, sales quotas, unfair labor practices, unfair management practices, not to mention nasty clientele…all add up to a wonderful growing experience if we look at it properly!

I do not believe in accidents, but in a wonderful, all-powerful, all-knowing, ever-present heavenly Father who loves me. In His great love and mercy He adds difficult people into my life and workplace for my benefit. The crashes are in every direction and almost every minute of every day. God in His great mercy allows these to happen for my growth. I can learn from them, or resist them. God promised a few things to me when I became one of His children:

> *"But we all, with unveiled face, beholding as in a mirror the glory of the Lord, are being transformed into the same image from glory to glory, just as from the Lord, the Spirit." 2 Corinthians 3:18 (NASB)*

> *"Being confident of this, that he who began a good work in you will carry it on to completion until the day of Christ Jesus." Philippians 1:6 (NIV)*

God is changing me from "one degree of glory to another degree of glory". Now we often get bogged down in the "to" part, between glories! But God is faithful to His word and His work. God promised to complete the work He began in me and He will do it. One of the quickest ways for God to accomplish His goal is to put me in pressure situations and let the junk of my life come bubbling up so it can be discovered and removed.

Work for many of us provides just the pressure we need to promote change in us. Harsh bosses and/or disagreeable

Dr. Jeffrey A. Klick

work associates are a perfect refining tool in the hands of the Master. As we go through our workday and crash into others, change takes place. We are often heated and sharpened without even knowing it. Do you think your network simply crashed and you lost all of your hard work by accident? No, God allows such things to help you grow. God loves you and will use everyone in your life to help accomplish His will for you. We can learn to enjoy the ride or spend our life complaining, but bumps and crashes will come either way.

Our spouse, children, grandchildren, in-laws, friends and work associates are some of God's most useful tools to help refine, shape, and mold us. God will use each and every situation to draw people to Himself and to fulfill His plan. We must change the way we look at these conflicts to be able to see God's shaping hand in our life to truly benefit from these close encounters!

Bumping into Your Church Family

The Family of God – you would think that the children of such a perfect Father could get along. However, we all know of church splits, politics, in-fighting, out-fighting, and general overall dissatisfaction within the house of God. King David had the proper perspective on the people of God.

> "As for the saints who are in the land, they are the glorious ones in whom is all my delight." Psalm 16:3 (NIV)

Believers are often called saints in the Scripture, and here even called glorious ones and David goes so far as to say they are his delight. Many of us simply struggle to put up with our brother and sisters in Christ, but to this king they were his delight! The next time you are with God's people, look around you and think, "these are the glorious ones" and "these are my delight." Now, that may be a stretch for some, especially if you are having a hard time with Sister Sandpaper, or Brother Braggart, but these folks are dearly loved by their Heavenly Father, and we also must love them.

God could remove any and all of our problems in a moment of time, but He doesn't because He has a bigger purpose in mind. God, in His perfect wisdom, often places very irritating people in our lives to help conform us to His Son's image and likeness. We will spend our entire lives on this earth bumping into our brothers and sisters that are also "works" in process. We grow to realize that each one is being shaped by the Master's hand and remember that they too are a work in process. And we must remember that we are often a tool in the Master's hand in their lives as well. We may be the very person that God is using to irritate, err, bump into another!

As we walk in the Way with other masterpieces in progress, we must learn to watch our words and make sure we speak life to each other.

"A word fitly spoken is like apples of gold in settings of silver." Proverbs 25:11

Dr. Jeffrey A. Klick

> *"Death and life are in the power of the tongue, and those who love it will eat its fruits." Proverbs 18:21*

These two verses give a sampling of the power that our words can impart. Sometimes in our encounters with other believers we speak just the right word – a golden apple, and other times, well, our words can have the odor of death in them. But our God is a wonderful, faithful Father who will not let us fail. When we fall short on a test, He simply reworks the timing and gives us the test again. In fact, He will continue to give us the same test until we pass it. We all work at our own pace, but we all will pass.

The Bride of Christ (the Church) is full of individual members, yet is one Body. All are needed and all provide a great opportunity for bumping! God uses our brothers and sisters in Christ to speak into our lives. These fellow believers in Christ are closer to us than any other people on the face of the earth for we have the same Father. Distance, race or creed makes little difference. I have traveled to China, Mexico, Nicaragua, the Philippines, and across the USA, and whenever you encounter a true believer, there is something inside of you that comes alive. Often you can tell who is a believer from across the room without ever talking to them. Everyone is unique and is loved by our Father. And since we are family, we can learn and grow by interaction.

Elders, deacons, ushers, pastors, choir members, worship team leaders, nursery workers, and a host of other titles are all potential crash partners. God places these folks in our lives to help us and to sharpen us. We can grow to love each other as we realize that God loves each one of us and therefore all have value. Even people that irritate us are there for a reason. God will use the weak and the strong to help us grow. We can comfort the weak and learn from the strong. If we do not give into envy or jealousy we will grow to appreciate the gifting in others and not be threatened by them.

It seems that many of us are very good at playing mind readers. We are sure we know exactly *why* someone did or said what he or she spoke or did. I call it assigning motives. The truth is most of do not know the motives of other people; we make a guess based on how *we* are feeling. We make 100% conclusions on 1% or less information, in many cases, and are often later proved very wrong in what we concluded. If we could move to giving each other the benefit of the doubt in the same way that we want people to give it to us, we would stop many arguments and hurtful situations before they break out. Think about that person that walked right by you on Sunday and didn't even acknowledge you, for example. It could be that they really *don't* like you or never have. And, it is possible that they do think they *are* better than you. They *may really* dislike your hair and clothes and it is also a possibility that they just left a conversation talking badly about you. Or…it could be that they just received some disturbing news. Or, they were in very deep thought about something, or they were on a mission to accomplish some very important task, or their mind was a million miles away from here…The truth is you do not know. Assigning them motives of why they ignored you will only cause pain, insecurity, and mistrust. Placing

Dr. Jeffrey A. Klick

yourself in their situation as if you were the one walking by might give you a totally different view!

Asking them the next time you see them, about what was going through their minds, might be a better solution than assigning them bad motives. Our enemy loves to work in the arena of darkness, suspicion, and accusation. He is called the "Accuser of the Brethren" for good reason, and the Devil does not need our assistance to stir up things!

Learning how to bump into to our brothers and sisters in Christ takes a lifetime. In one way or another we are all very sensitive people. We can be hurt, slighted, overlooked, and under loved by just about anyone. We must learn how to bump into each other in a gracious way. As we become part of a Body of believers we will have ample opportunity to grow in our bumping skills! Soon, someone in our church family will disappoint us; many will irritate us, and all will crash into us at some point or another. This is the way God has designed the Church to work. The Church is full of people learning how to put His love into practice.

When I become discouraged at what I see in the Church I recall this verse and it helps greatly.

> *"And I tell you that you are Peter and on this rock I will build my church, and the gates of Hades will not overcome it. Matthew 16:18 (NIV)*

God is the One that will build the Church. Not me; not you; God said *He* would build. And if the Church is His Bride (Revelation 21:2), and if He is coming back for a Bride without spot or wrinkle (Ephesians 5:27) then God has much work to complete! His people learning how to crash into each other will help accomplish much of that work! As we learn how to interact with each other in the Church, we can and will help each other become more like Christ.

Bumping into Strangers

As if it were not enough to have a spouse, children, friends, work associates, and church folks to crash into, there is a whole great big world of people just waiting for our impact! One of my annual treats is to watch the movie "*It's a Wonderful Life.*" Along with millions of others this is part of our Christmas tradition. As the story unfolds George Bailey is given an opportunity that most of us would love to have – to see how our world would really be without our impact. George is allowed to see how his friends, family, and town would have developed without his seemingly insignificant contribution.

George always struggled to see how his little meaningless life had any value or worth. But after a very short time of seeing the void left without his life, he cries to be back to his drab little world. As Clarence the angel so aptly puts it – "each one of our lives touches so many others." Many of those touches (crashes) go unrealized and are rarely appreciated if we do grasp them at all.

We all bump into so many folks during a typical week - clerks, fellow drivers, phone callers, neighbors, shoppers, and dozens of others that are mostly just part of the scenery. Yet, without any realization on our part we bump

Dr. Jeffrey A. Klick

into them. How we smile or don't smile at the checkout line; how we drive through the parking lot or down the highway; how we even answer the phone; how we treat the server at the restaurant and how we tip; how we walk or drive through our neighborhood; and hundreds of other such encounters happen every week and we are oblivious to the potential.

The Scripture also adds a little spice to this whole stranger thing.

> *"Do not forget to entertain strangers, for by so doing some people have entertained angels without knowing it." Hebrews 13:2 (NIV)*

Now some will argue that angels can be translated messengers and that is fine. The point is that whether it is a heavenly being or simply a messenger on duty for heaven, it matters how we bump them! How we crash into these strangers is important in God's kingdom and our personal growth.

Each encounter we have with people is a potential life-changing opportunity. God knows what each person needs at any given moment and He will use each one of us to help move people in the proper direction. He loves us enough to bring people into our lives for the same purpose. As we begin to change how we look at these "chance" encounters, we will see more of God's hand in them.

Let's Be Purposeful:

If it is true that we will spend our days bumping into each other, then the obvious question is which direction will we push people? After impact with us, will they move towards godliness and spiritual growth or away from the Lord and His purposes? My challenge is to realize that I will crash into countless people in my day and my goal is to push them to Christ. Words, smiles, actions and reactions can nudge people closer to God. When I interact with my spouse and children my goal is to help them see Jesus in my life. Outbursts of anger or pampering my ego will not accomplish this goal. Having to be right in everything or always getting my way will not help. But, learning to embrace the power of the cross, taking the road of humility, and esteeming everyone as better than me will help accomplish the goal of bumping people towards Jesus.

Powerful words like "you were right, I was wrong, please forgive me" will help bump towards the Lord. Learning not to jump to conclusions and assigning motives to family, friends, church family, and co-workers will also help. Growing to appreciate the differences in people instead of being threatened by them is another good goal. Reaching out to the lost or unlovely will certainly help in this growth process. Doing random acts of kindness expecting nothing in return will help push people the right direction. Guarding my heart from anger and bitterness keeps my "bumping" under control, "for the anger of man does not accomplish the purposes of God" - (James 1:20)

Dr. Jeffrey A. Klick

and "roots of bitterness will simply defile many." – (Hebrews 12:15)

Before I end, let me ask you a question; "How do you smell?" Well, you might say "Humph! That is a personal question." What I mean is this:

> *"For we are the aroma of Christ to God among those who are being saved and among those who are perishing, to one a fragrance from death to death, to the other a fragrance from life to life."*
> *2 Corinthians 2:15-16*

While not probing these two verses too deeply, the basic thought is that we have an aroma when we interact with people. Are we a sweet-smelling fragrance that people miss after we are gone, or are we a bitter, repugnant odor that people wish they had never encountered? Jesus has been called the "Rose of Sharon". I bet He "smelled" really good!

All of this bumping and crashing into people can give me a headache, unless I can learn to see these events from God's perspective. God's plan for His people has been described as looking at the back of a huge tapestry. From the backside all we can see is a mess of threads going everywhere with no pattern or discernible shape. But when we step around the other side we can see the finished work and marvel at its beauty. God alone sees the big picture and He is the one doing the work. God places each thread just where He wants it to go and we rarely get to see the other side of the work. We must take it on faith that the finished product looks good and one day when this life is through and we step through the veil into eternity our perspective will be clear.

No matter where we are in the process or how good or bad we may feel we have done, it is God's view that matters. God has supplied everything that is needed to be successful in this life (2 Peter 1:3). If we have failed in some way then we go to the cross, repent and receive the forgiveness granted by the blood of Jesus. Then we start over again. As we rise each day His mercies are new and we can climb again into that seat, strap on our seatbelt and start looking for someone to crash into!

Questions to Consider:

1. Is my life a series of unrelated accidents, or is God really working in all of my daily events and personal contacts?

2. Does God really have "works" for me to complete? Am I really His masterpiece?

3. Is my value system the same as Gods? How do I know?

Chapter Four - We all Stand on Something

If the foundations are destroyed, what can the righteous do? Psalm 11:3

The psalmist David asks this question and it is worth exploring. Most of us do not have to think too hard to realize that our society is in big trouble. Marriages are being destroyed, all manner of hideous crimes are being committed by even young children, moral restraint is almost unheard of, and evil seems to be winning the day. The daily news we may watch via TV or internet is mostly a depressing gathering of stories revealing that the foundations are cracked and ready to crumble into a pile of dust! "What can the righteous do?" is an excellent question.

A good beginning for our reply is to recognize the root problems. "Why" is a question that needs to be asked. Why are we in this condition? Why are marriages falling apart and being rapidly replaced with cohabitation and alternate lifestyles? Why are young children becoming violent and callous? Why is the Church seemingly ineffective? One of the benefits of getting older is that we realize that we no longer have, or need to have all of the answers to every question. It is true that there are many possible answers to the questions posed, and any simple response will be incomplete. However, that does not mean we should not attempt to look at these questions and pursue a different course of action than what is currently being followed. Even though we cannot do or understand everything, we should do something!

Dr. Jeffrey A. Klick

Many individual lives and societies fall apart because storms hit and they are unprepared or never dream that tragedy could happen to them. History shows that nations often reject God and replace Him with other gods like money, power, humanism, and a host of other idols. Each of these false gods pretend to provide a solid foundation but the storms test their ability. What can be shaken will be and that is a promise from the one, true God.

> *At that time his voice shook the earth, but now he has promised, "Yet once more I will shake not only the earth but also the heavens. This phrase, "Yet once more," indicates the removal of things that are shaken—that is, things that have been made—in order that the things that cannot be shaken may remain. Therefore let us be grateful for receiving a kingdom that cannot be shaken, and thus let us offer to God acceptable worship, with reverence and awe. Hebrews 12:26-28*

Hard times hit everyone and how we stand will be directly tied to what our foundation is built upon. Nations that build upon sand will fare no better than individuals who do the same. Jesus put it this way:

> *"Everyone then who hears these words of mine and does them will be like a wise man who built his house on the rock. And the rain fell, and the floods came, and the winds blew and beat on that house, but it did not fall, because it had been founded on the rock. And everyone who hears these words of*

mine and does not do them will be like a foolish
man who built his house on the sand. And the rain
fell, and the floods came, and the winds blew and
beat against that house, and it fell, and great was
the fall of it." Matthew 7:24-27

Rain, wind and floods come to everyone, but destruction is tied to our foundation. If we are building upon the Rock, we will stand. If we build upon the foundation of any other god, we will fall. "Other gods" come in many shapes and disguises. I already referred to money, power, and human reasoning. How about greed, selfishness, false religion, pride, judgmentalism, legalism, secularism and having a temporal focus, to name a few. Building our lives upon these foundations of sand will not stand the test of storms.

We do not want to build on these false gods so what should we build upon? The answer resides in two passages that I already quoted. There is a kingdom that cannot be shaken and Jesus said that if His words are heard, and *acted upon,* we would stand in the time of the storm. Simply put we must be those that obey Jesus and have as our main desire, the furthering of His Kingdom. Most of us are familiar with these words and concepts, but walking them out is a different matter. Let us consider two very important passages:

But seek first the kingdom of God and his
righteousness, and all these things will be added to
you. Matthew 6:33

Dr. Jeffrey A. Klick

> *Whoever has my commandments and keeps them, he it is who loves me. John 14:21*

If we are "seeking first the kingdom of God" then whatever else there may be in our life must take a lower place. There cannot be two first places. Seeking God with all of our heart, all of our soul, and our entire mind, as we are commanded in multiple places, suggests that this pursuit must be all encompassing. We proclaim that Jesus is Lord, and this is good and right. How often have we stopped to consider what that really means? As I have already shared, lordship is an exclusive title and claim. There cannot be two supreme lords ruling in our lives at the same time, for one must take preeminence over the other. Jesus said we cannot serve God and money and we cannot have two lords sitting on the throne of our life either.

The "lord" who is currently on the throne of my life will be the one making the decisions regarding what I do, how I spend my time and money, where I go, what I say, etc. If my focus is on how to advance the Kingdom of God, then my actions will be directed in a very different path than if I were advancing the kingdom of Jeff. If I am in service to my King Jesus, then He promises that all the other things of life will be taken care of for me. That does not mean that I remove myself from society or become a slacker, for that would reflect poorly on my King. Instead, I strive to become the best worker, best father, best husband, and best whatever because I am promoting my Lord's Kingdom. How I live reflects on my King.

Couple this building block with Jesus' words stating who it is that really loves Him, and I begin to see what I

should do in order to stand in the face of storms. I must
seek the Kingdom and begin to understand what the King is
commanding. If my King really is The King, then whatever
He may allow into my life will be for the ultimate good. If
my King really is the Sovereign Lord of the universe, then
what escapes His notice? My King said:

> *Are not two sparrows sold for a penny? And not one
> of them will fall to the ground apart from your
> Father. But even the hairs of your head are all
> numbered. Fear not, therefore; you are of more
> value than many sparrows. Matthew 10:29-31*

God knows all, sees all, understands all, is all-powerful,
all wise, all loving, and that is just the tip of our
understanding of our Lord. If all that is true, then as His
child, I can stand in the midst of the storms of life that He
allows. If I do not believe these things then what do I
possibly build upon that will stand against the ravages of
pain, heartache, loss, and despair? Many state that we
Christians use God as a crutch and they do not know the
half of it. God is the only reason we stand. Our faith is the
reason we can walk in this sin-laden world with all of its
heartaches, pain and death and still smile. We know that
not only will we survive, but also we will overcome. We
are serving a God that cannot be moved, and serve in His
Kingdom that cannot be shaken. Our foundation is sound,
strong, and will endure forever.

We know these beliefs to be true because we trust in
God's Word. God has revealed some of Who He is and
what He does in the Scriptures and we take these truths to

heart. God either is Who He said He was, or He is not. If He is not, then nothing else really matters. But, if He is Who He said He was, then everything changes. He said He is the Sovereign Lord of the universe, and He has a will and He issues commands. We who have bowed our knee to Him will attempt to follow those commands empowered by His grace. If God allows, better stated, *when* He allows trouble, heartache, suffering, disappointment, and such, we bow before Him and give Him our praise. He is God and He can do whatever He wants, whenever He wants, in whatever way He wants. If He is truly good, loves us, and has a master plan, we can trust Him and worship Him even when we do not understand much of it. This understanding makes for very firm ground to stand on in the midst of storms.

By contrast, building upon the opinions of men, material possessions or ourselves will always lead to collapse of our foundation. People will disappoint us and they are fickle, we will fail personally in some fashion, and every temporal possession will be left behind when we leave this life. Building our life on any of these three will ultimately lead to ruin when life's trouble hits. Jesus promised that storms would assault our house; what are we building upon? Let us look just a bit more at these three possible foundations in contrast to building upon Jesus and His Word.

People are made in the image of God and are to be loved. In fact, we are told in many places that how we love others is a pretty good picture of how we love God. However, loved is different from worshipped, idolized, and used as a foundation. Building our lives based on how we are treated or viewed by others will lead to a shaky building. "What have you done for me lately?" is a pretty common statement in reference to people. People can love us one day and forsake us the next. Jesus certainly understood this for He said He did not entrust Himself to men for He knew what was in the heart of men - John 2:24. We would be wise to follow Jesus' example. We are to love one another, serve one another, even if necessary, die one for another, but not worship one another or find our worth and value in the opinions of others. Every person is a fellow pilgrim on the journey of life; they are not deity and should not be elevated to such a position. There is only room for one Lord and that must be Jesus.

Worshipping others is not healthy and neither is elevating ourselves to the place reserved for God. Self, in our day, is idolized. We are told via most media outlets, counselors, and internally that we are number one. We deserve to be pampered, treated better than we are, and to take care of ourselves first and foremost. After thirty years of marriage counseling one phrase is said over and over to me in my office, "I need to think about me, and take care of me for awhile," as if being selfish is a novelty. Variations of this sentiment are, "I just want to be happy." "God wants me happy." and, "If I don't take care of me I can't be any good to anyone else." There is just enough truth in these sentences to almost always deceive someone.

The Scriptures never state any of the above concepts but present a radically different approach:

Then Jesus told his disciples, "If anyone would come after me, let him deny himself and take up his cross and follow me. Matthew 16:24

Dr. Jeffrey A. Klick

> *Whoever does not bear his own cross and come*
> *after me cannot be my disciple. Luke 14:27*

The Biblical principle is death to self, not seek the welfare of self. Self-control is a fruit of the Holy Spirit and selfishness is a weed from of our old, carnal nature. When we confuse these two truths, we have begun to believe a lie.

In addition to crucifying ourselves, we are told to treat others in the following fashion:

> *Do nothing from rivalry or conceit, but in humility*
> *count others more significant than yourselves. Let*
> *each of you look not only to his own interests, but*
> *also to the interests of others. Philippians 2:3-4*

While we all have personal needs, our main focus is to be outwardly seeking the benefit of others. Christianity always moves us away from ourselves and towards seeking the welfare of others, and this is especially true regarding those who are the closest to us. When we attempt to build our lives upon a foundation of selfishness, our building will not stand when the raging rain and winds descend.

I mentioned that building our lives upon temporal possessions will not help us during the rough times above, and many can testify to this truth. Everything we own and all we see will someday be left behind when we die. If the Lord comes back to take us home with Him, then all these earthly items will also be left behind. Building our lives on houses, land, money, and pleasure will lead to a shaky foundation. In a moment's time all of these things can be taken away. Car accidents, health breakdowns, stock market crashes, and a host of other events that we have no control over can change our lives in a moment.

One example will show what I mean. I worked for many years for an extremely busy man. He sat in my office one day with his head in his hands bemoaning that he did not have one appointment open for the next six months. Meeting after meeting filled his calendar with no end in sight. Shortly after he was in my office, he received word that his wife had cancer and he instantly cleared every one of those meetings. All of those seemingly unavoidable meetings were simply cancelled when something *more* important came on the scene. This experience always reminds me that we need to make sure we are placing the proper emphasis on the issues that really matter. Life is full of surprises and if we construct our foundation with materials that are destined to perish, we are not very wise.

We all are building our lives on something; only buildings constructed with eternal materials will stand the tests of time and life's storms. We must look at our lives and choose Jesus and His Words, for anything less than this is destined to fail. As we build with God's Word, His grace, and enabled by the power of His Holy Spirit, our lives will become a living epistle known and read by many others. As we walk through the guaranteed trials of this life what, or perhaps better stated, Who will sustain us? We are invited by Jesus to abide in Him and in His Word, and if we take Him up on His offer, we will stand.

In addition to the storms of life, we also have enemies that want to take us down. In the next chapter I want us to discover the battle we all face and how to not only survive,

Dr. Jeffrey A. Klick

but also win. Before leaving this chapter pause a minute or two and prayerfully consider these questions.

Questions to Consider:

1. What foundation am I building my life upon? Scripture? Money? People?

2. Is Jesus still Lord even during the storms that are in my life?

3. What does Jesus being Lord of my life mean in my daily living?

Chapter Five - Three Common Foes

We should not picnic in the midst of falling bombs.

"Know thy foe" is an ancient proverb that is not only battle tested, but is also a practical piece of wisdom. The Scripture reveals that we have three primary enemies:

> *You adulterous people! Do you not know that friendship with the world is enmity with God? Therefore whoever wishes to be a friend of the world makes himself an enemy of God. James 4:4*

> *For those who live according to the flesh set their minds on the things of the flesh, but those who live according to the Spirit set their minds on the things of the Spirit. For to set the mind on the flesh is death, but to set the mind on the Spirit is life and peace. For the mind that is set on the flesh is hostile to God, for it does not submit to God's law; indeed, it cannot. Romans 8:5-7*

> *Be sober-minded; be watchful. Your adversary the devil prowls around like a roaring lion, seeking someone to devour. 1 Peter 5:8*

The world, the flesh, and the devil are well known enemies to our spiritual growth and survival, yet we often tend to forget that we are even in a battle. In the early 1970's a friend of mine used to sing this corny song about, "It's a battlefield brother not a picnic that God has called us

Dr. Jeffrey A. Klick

to." However, in my experience as a pastor for over 30 years and a believer since 1973, that song has proved to be absolutely correct. Often we act as if we are sitting on a hill with our red and white checkered tablecloth spread with picnic goodies and are oblivious to the bombs and warfare going on all around us! We are worried about ants when we should be looking for flaming darts.

Our churches and families are not unaware, however, at least to the damage caused. Divorce is rampant. Young people are leaving the faith in droves. Verbal and physical abuse is becoming common even in Christian marriages. Immorality among pastors, as well as their members, must be near an all time high. The Church seems to be ineffective against the destruction of the family and the decay slowly taking over society, and offers little hope to those that have real trouble. Instead of offering solutions to marital breakdowns, poverty, sickness, homelessness, and a host of other issues, we delegate our duties to the government and secular counselors. To be completely fair, general statements are broad sweeping by design and those two previous sentences are also. There are pockets within the Church that are making a huge difference in the lives of many people and they should not only be commended but imitated, however, just about every major study points to the Church losing ground in Her effectiveness. We simply are not all that salty anymore, and our light in the darkness is not bright!

Moving from sweeping generalizations to where we live is probably more helpful. I cannot do anything about the overall condition of the Church at large; in fact, it is not my responsibility for Jesus said He would build His Church.

He can and will do a much better job than you or I. What I can do is focus on my realm of authority and influence, and I can challenge you to do the same!

How is my marriage going? Is my marriage presenting an image of oneness in the fashion of Christ and the Church? How are we doing in raising the next generation for Christ? What kind of employee or employer am I? Do I walk in moral purity daily? What would those that know me best say about my walk with God? After I leave a meeting or group of people, are they glad I left or wish that I had stayed longer? What is coming out of my mouth on a regular basis? Whom have I helped today? There are many more questions that could be asked, but those are enough to make my point. We all have plenty to ask God to help us with and we can leave the bigger issues in His competent hands. Most of us do not have a knowledge problem, we have an obedience problem. We already know far more than we are currently willing to do.

If any of those questions above prompted a squirm then you are probably normal, for they should make us uncomfortable. We all instinctively know that we have problems and we need to grow. My appeal to you and to myself is to remember that we are in a battle with real enemies and they want to destroy us. I will start with the last of the three I mentioned:

For we do not wrestle against flesh and blood, but against the rulers, against the authorities, against the cosmic powers over this present darkness, against the spiritual forces of evil in the heavenly places. Ephesians 6:12

The apostle Paul reveals our real enemy in this verse and it is hard for me to remember this truth when I am not getting along with others. This is especially true when my wife and I fuss for it is easy to forget this verse. At the moment of our "intense fellowship", her flesh is greatly annoying my flesh and it takes a huge effort to even think about spiritual warfare! With Paul's words in mind though, we must step back and see a bigger picture. Disagreements are perfectly normal between couples; moving to divorce court is not. Irritations provide us opportunities for growth in the fruit of the Spirit, but our foe desires that these issues become full-blown sores that fester into a terminal illness for our relationships. Stopping long enough in the midst of conflict to pray, ask the Holy Spirit to give insight, check my motives, and recognize the enemy's activity will help in this battle. Ignoring or failing to realize that there is a spiritual side to everything is dangerous. In every conflict there are three wills involved: the humans, our enemy, and God's. We must seek God's will, resist our enemy, and die to our self if we hope to mature and become effective for our Lord. As we grasp this truth we become battled tested and successes will become the norm. Failures simply point to a need for reinforcement and more training.

Earlier I referenced Peter's warning to be sober minded and on guard for our adversary the devil prowls around like a roaring lion seeking someone to devour. Lions are huge predators not to be taken lightly. Peter issues the warning because there is real danger and multiple church studies reveal the damage. We must learn to resist our foe so that he flees from us. We must learn what it means to put on the armor God has provided as explained in Ephesians 6. We also need to learn how to use our weapons that Paul shares with us here:

> *For though we walk in the flesh, we are not waging war according to the flesh. For the weapons of our warfare are not of the flesh but have divine power to destroy strongholds. We destroy arguments and every lofty opinion raised against the knowledge of God, and take every thought captive to obey Christ. 2 Corinthians 10:3-5*

The battle primarily rages between our ears and therein is the solution as well. We learn to renew our minds with the truth of God's Word. "Strongholds" is a word that has the concept of lies and falsehoods in it and the only way to effectively fight and defeat lies is with truth. "Thy Word is truth," the Scriptures proclaim and Jesus said that He was truth. Any hint of lying is not of the same cloth. Any shades of falsehood have no place in the life of a follower of the One that proclaimed He was truth personified. We are to wage war and we have armor and weapons to be successful. At least part of the problem is we forget to fight the correct enemy.

This is not meant to be an exhaustive resource on spiritual warfare so I will move on to the next enemy that desires to see us fail. This one is a bit harder to deal with since it is so personal. The ancients always lumped together these three foes - the world, the flesh and the devil. We have briefly looked at the devil, so keeping in reverse order; let us talk about our flesh.

Dr. Jeffrey A. Klick

Flesh is a term having nothing to do with skin, but everything to do with our nature. When we are born again, we become new creations in Christ, yet there is a part of us that still lingers. Theologians argue over whether the old nature is the flesh or does the new nature just retain a memory of our old before Christ life. I will gladly allow them to continue the debate. The reality is no matter what you call it, we all struggle with daily decisions to walk in obedience. Our flesh rises up and challenges God's call to holiness, purity, death-to-self, esteeming others as better than our self, humility, rejoicing in others' success and prosperity, and many other issues. Most honest Christians will state that they battle their fleshly desires on a minute-by-minute basis.

Paul gives us insight here as well in this exchange:

> *For I do not understand my own actions. For I do not do what I want, but I do the very thing I hate. Now if I do what I do not want, I agree with the law, that it is good. So now it is no longer I who do it, but sin that dwells within me. For I know that nothing good dwells in me, that is, in my flesh. For I have the desire to do what is right, but not the ability to carry it out. For I do not do the good I want, but the evil I do not want is what I keep on doing. Romans 7:15-19*

Who has not spent a great deal of prayer time crying out just what Paul wrote? Regardless of what is finally revealed as to the source of our flesh, the battle is real. My flesh is not in step with my spirit regarding the desire to obey God.

My flesh must be trained, disciplined, and brought under subjection in order to walk in obedience to my Lord's commands. Left to itself, my flesh will always choose against what is righteous.

God knows this and has provided everything we need to succeed! We have the Word of God given to instruct us, correct us, lead us, train us, restrain us, and to change the way we think, and we have the Holy Spirit living right inside of us to teach us what it all means. Consider these familiar passages specifically regarding our flesh:

> *But the Helper, the Holy Spirit, whom the Father will send in my name, he will teach you all things and bring to your remembrance all that I have said to you. John 14:26*

> *For the word of God is living and active, sharper than any two-edged sword, piercing to the division of soul and of spirit, of joints and of marrow, and discerning the thoughts and intentions of the heart. Hebrews 4:12*

God knows we will struggle with sinful desires, selfish motives, and even choose harmful actions sometimes. By His infinite wisdom, He has provided the Word of God and the Holy Spirit to help equip each believer with a guidance system! We can know the truth and we can choose to walk in obedience to that truth. I do not believe we will ever be free of our flesh this side of eternity, but we can grow in grace and obtain a significant measure of victory over our flesh. By becoming students of the Word of God and by training our senses to listen to the promptings of the Holy Spirit inside of us, we can grow, mature, and walk in the fullness of Christ's victory! After all, learning to control our flesh is a fruit of the Spirit listed in Galatians 5:23, right alongside love, joy and peace.

The third enemy on the list is the world. The world in the Scriptures does not refer to our natural, visible surroundings, but to a prevailing philosophy that impacts everything. We tend to say that someone or some activity is worldly and by that, we mean it is not spiritual or perhaps holy. Biblically defined, a person that looks like, acts like and thinks likes those that are not of our Kingdom would be worldly. As believers in our Lord Jesus Christ, we are new creations in Him and our old way of life is dead. In water baptism we held a funeral service for that old way of life. We are no longer children of this world and we now have God as our Father, not our old father the devil. Everything has become new!

Our previous family is not happy about this fact and will work overtime to get us back into the fold. Temptations increase after we are born again, they do not go away. Often struggles and hardships become more pronounced when we change kingdoms. Why? We are in a war and our foe has lost someone to the Good guys. The Scripture is very clear on the battle and its severity:

> *And do not be conformed to this world, but be transformed by the renewing of your mind, so that you may prove what the will of God is, that which is good and acceptable and perfect. Romans 12:2*

See to it that no one takes you captive through philosophy and empty deception, according to the tradition of men, according to the elementary principles of the world, rather than according to Christ. Colossians 2:8

You adulteresses, do you not know that friendship with the world is hostility toward God? Therefore whoever wishes to be a friend of the world makes himself an enemy of God. James 4:4

Do not love the world nor the things in the world. If anyone loves the world, the love of the Father is not in him. For all that is in the world, the lust of the flesh and the lust of the eyes and the boastful pride of life, is not from the Father, but is from the world. 1 John 2:15-16

We know that we are of God, and that the whole world lies in the power of the evil one. 1 John 5:19

This sampling of verses should be sufficient to get our thoughts turning in the proper direction. We sometimes forget that behind every movie, TV show, book, song, and advertisement there is an underlying philosophy. The creators of these communication tools are attempting to forward a message to their audience. What is that message? We do not war against rocks and stones, rivers and trees, but against a mindset that is in direct opposition to God's. I am not opposed to any of these forms of communication; my appeal is simply that as believers we would not be

Dr. Jeffrey A. Klick

ignorant of the underlying messages being presented. If it is
possible to be conformed to the world, to be taken captive
to empty philosophy, to be a friend of the world, and to
love those things that God hates, then I must be aware of
what is going on around me, in me, and also in those for
which I am responsible, and do all I can to counter and
resist it.

Being worldly or giving into the spirit of this world is
not defined by a long list of what to do or not, but by what
underlying philosophy we adopt. Are we walking according
to the Laws of the Kingdom of God, or to the ones dictated
by the prince of the power of the air? (Ephesians 2:2) Is
there really such a thing as something being amoral?
Perhaps, but the creations of people are rooted in one or the
other Kingdom. Being blind to this is dangerous at best and
even possibly a spiritual disaster. We are not to be ignorant
of our enemy's schemes, but are we?

The world, flesh, and devil are real enemies that want to
destroy us. Will we fight? Will we train those under our
care to do battle? Will we prayerfully consider the Word of
God and what it says regarding our foe? If not, we are
headed for deception and defeat. If we will, the Scripture
promises us effective weapons, divine armor, and ultimate
victory! Study it out yourself and see if what I shared was
true. I promise you that I only scratched the surface. Dig
deep. Enter the battle. Win the war.

Questions to Consider:

1. How am I really doing in spiritual warfare? Gaining or losing ground?

2. Does my flesh rule my daily life or Jesus and His commandments?

3. Have I given into the world system around me in some way?

4. Am I ready to get into the fight with the world, my flesh and the devil? If not, why not?

Chapter Six: Unheralded Powerful Servants

First glances are often very wrong.

I first thought about this chapter as I listened to my friend Dennis share his personal testimony. It was a listing of people that had made a difference in his life and it was powerful! We all like to receive approval and positive comments. In fact, God knows we need the affirmation, so after this life He says, "Well done, good and faithful servant," to those that have followed Him in obedience. What follows is a partial listing of people that have interacted in my life and helped me along the journey. I hope after you read this chapter you will take a moment and think about those that have helped you along in your journey. If you are able, perhaps you could drop someone a note of thanks sharing what they meant to you. It might mean the world to them!

Your life and mine may not have intersected yet, but you and I both have others we have impacted, and, Lord willing, there are many more opportunities ahead before we leave this life. Every person is important and each interaction has the potential to leave a lasting impression. Space prohibits me from listing everyone, but I trust that we can learn from this partial listing of people that I have been blessed to know! God places people in our life for a reason, and I have included some of the lessons I learned in life from others that God sent my way. You have your own list and you are on other's lists. My desire is to make it on many other's lists before I die, and maybe after you read this chapter, you will have the same goal.

Leslie

Yes, this is the same Leslie in the opening pages of this book. My companion from youth, my bride, my love, my partner in everything, has been making an impact in my life for almost forty years. Not only is she my wife but she is a tremendous example to me and demonstrates a thoughtful, caring for others that rarely enters my mind. While there are many of her character traits I could share with you, let me pick just one or two for our purpose. Leslie has a passion for compassion and sensitivity that makes me look like a rock in comparison. Leslie deeply cares for other people's feelings and their well-being. She is by far the most "others" sensitive person I know.

A small example to illustrate this is Leslie's uncanny ability to hear one time what someone likes or dislikes and remember it forever. If, in a casual conversation someone says, "I like baked potatoes, and not boiled," Leslie will remember this and only serve them baked if we have them over to share a meal, even years later. The same would be true for outfits, colors, soda preference, and just about anything that someone would mention. She cares deeply for, and wants to please others and this is just a small example of how she does it. She listens to what people express and remembers it. She focuses on what they like and commits it to memory. A small thing, yet it captures the essence of how Leslie thinks. She values others and cares about what they think and desire.

My wife, while not really happy with me for using her as an example because she prefers to stay in the background, is a servant and giver unlike anyone else I know. She is almost never too busy or too tired to meet a legitimate need. Over the years, she has helped me soften up quite a bit, to take more care with what I say, and to consider other people's feelings. With my personality, these were all new concepts, and while I am not complete yet, I am growing!

On occasion, after leaving a group of people, Leslie will reveal to me many of the potential feeling type issues that I overlooked. "Did you notice Jane sitting there by herself?" Or, "Sue didn't smile once tonight, I hope everything is alright." "Did you see Bob's expression change when you made fun of him?" Ouch. Of course not, that would require paying attention to someone other than myself! The compassion and empathy for others that my bride expresses naturally, challenges my harshness and self-focus to the core.

God knew what I needed in a lifelong companion and He gave me a jewel. Once I quit fighting the differences and began to embrace them as God's gifts (by the way, this skill has not been perfected yet!) growth came. God did not intend for my wife and I to be twins, but two unique people that interact with each other and foster growth, maturity, and change. Most of us have wondered why we married opposite type personalities. Does God just have some sort of warped sense of humor or does He really have a plan? In my life, His plan has been furthered by interacting with a wonderful, gracious, giving lady named Leslie, and for this gift I am eternally grateful. I can and should learn from this strength that she possesses. How I treat people matters. Do I listen with an ear of a servant? Do I really care how *they* feel, what *they* are going through, or what *they* think? Do I think about how my humor would hurt the person I am using as a laugh opportunity? Shouldn't I?

Please do not get me wrong, Leslie, or for that matter, any of these people mentioned are just people. They are not perfect or even necessarily exceptionally gifted in some way. They are just like you and me, and that is the point! Super gifted people are often hard to relate to, but these folks helped change my life by just being human and caring. We can all do the same for others and never put on the cape of the superhero!

Craig

I became a Christian between my junior and senior year of high school. The cliques were very well defined in those days and you generally fit into a single category and did not intermix. I was part of the longhaired, drugged up, freak culture up until my salvation. We met every day and listened to loud music, smoked, participated in illegal activities, and stayed away from the jocks, greasers and Christian kids. After I met the Lord, I was completely displaced. Leslie attended a different high school and my dope-smoking buddies soon grew very tired of my new ways. I still had long hair and was way too rough for the Christian group. It was a lonely time for me because even Christ's kids can be hurtful by leaving out someone that is different. I was still very different.

One day a rather unique young man approached me and began to talk about the Lord. Craig really did not fit into any grouping and I found this interesting. He simply did not care about such things. He loved Jesus and if you did, that was good enough for him. Craig took me under his wing and befriended this new babe in Christ. We spent a great deal of time together talking about the things of God and why they mattered. Craig was an excellent piano player so we often would go to his house and sing. These were wonderful times. Most of my daily life was consumed with working and my relationship with Leslie, but Craig was always there for me when needed. He did not require much friendship wise, and looking back, he did not get much from me. I was the needy one, and he met that need without requiring anything from me in return.

I learned from this young man that judging the outside of someone is often premature and many times very wrong. I was still a mess in my outside appearance and probably scared most of the Christian kids, but not Craig. He just showed me the love of Christ and it laid an excellent brick in my foundation. Craig eventually married and went on to spend some time in Turkey serving the Lord with his bride.

May I learn how to love and reach out to people that do not readily fit into my box, like my friend Craig. I pray that I can also learn how to hold friendships with a loose grip, for maybe they are there for only a short season to help lay a brick in the foundation.

Harry

In my early employment days before becoming a pastor, I was a District Manager for a national tax firm. Actually, my title was Satellite Franchise Director, but that is simply a detail. Before being hired by the Block brothers, I was swinging a hammer and doing remodeling. Okay, that is not quite accurate either. I was great at demolition and not so hot at reconstruction. I decided that ripping out bug-infested walls was not going to be a long-term career, so on a whim I took a tax course with the hopes of entering management.

During the interview with the stern looking HR person, I expressed my desire to stay on with the company after the tax season. The answer went something like, good luck because we go from over 100 employees down to two! The odds sounded about right to me so I took the job. After a very productive tax season, I was offered an assistant manager's position in Wichita, Kansas. My wife and I drove down there several times looking for housing and left each time frustrated. On the final drive back, I saw my bride looking out the window with a tear running down her cheek. I called up the folks offering me the job and told them I could not accept it. They said too bad, so sad, do not call us anymore, and hung up. So that was the end of my dream.

Or so I thought. After several more weeks of swinging that hammer at cockroaches, I received a call from the tax folks. They asked if I would be willing to move to Cameron Missouri as the District Manager. I said, "Sure, where is Cameron?" Cameron was a small town about sixty miles north of where we lived and on our first trip there, we found a house. By turning down the job, I received a promotion and substantial raise! While I do not recommend that procedure, God often works in mysterious ways.

In our new town, the first order of business was to find a local church. Since my office was a few doors down from the local Christian bookstore, I stopped in and began to ask some questions. In a town of about 4,000, everyone pretty much knew everything about anyone, so getting information was easy. As God would have it, the family that owned the bookstore went to a sister church from the one we had left to move to Cameron, so we had found both a physical home and a spiritual one.

Within a month or two, the honeymoon was over and a crisis hit within the church. There was a power struggle, the church split and the pastor left. While there is plenty of blame to go around, we went with the pastor and by process of elimination, I became his right-hand man. In fact, given the demographics of the church, I was about the only man. Harry took me under his wing and began to introduce me to ministry, study, and the pastoral lifestyle. This man that had never attended seminary had a brilliant mind. He taught himself Greek and was a very gifted teacher. His ability to make a pun from almost any word was incredible. We ended up moving from our original house in Cameron and rented a house that was next door to Harry and his lovely wife Judy, thus allowing our friendship to blossom.

Our relationship grew and I learned a great many life lessons from this godly couple. Judy was extremely proper and Harry was a cut-up. I learned that it was okay to be myself and that God could use me just the way I was. God would clean up and reform what was needed, but that was His job and He is extremely good at His work. I learned how to put together a sermon, visit the sick, teach in nursing homes, relate to all manner of people, counsel others and learn the general skills necessary for the life of a pastor. I had no intention of ever going into full time ministry, but again, God has His own will and ways!

I watched my friend Harry walk through difficult times and not lose his faith. He felt bitterly betrayed and abandoned, yet he walked on. I watched him with his wife and children and learned many lessons. Much of what Harry taught me was caught by simply being his friend. Life is like that. When it became time for us to leave Cameron, it was extremely hard because of our friendship.

We have stayed in touch over the years and Harry continues to amaze me. He still writes books even though has been forced to retire from speaking due to Parkinson's Disease. And, he still encourages me to continue on in my calling. His lovely bride has died and his children have had their struggles, but Harry continues to be a faithful man of God. Only heaven will reveal the full impact of his life on others, and the influence he had on my life. Harry was willing to trust me, empower me, and take a risk with me. May my life be thought of that way by other young men that God has His hand upon for service. Help me Lord to see potential and not just the weaknesses in others.

Malcolm

I only met Malcolm twice in my life, but I spent hundreds of hours with him via the wonder of cassette tapes! If you do not know what a cassette is then look it up on the web. Part of my job in Cameron was to drive all over North Missouri and on into Southern Iowa and visit the franchise offices. Leslie and I also took care of the tape library for our church so I would grab a handful of tapes and begin my eight-hour trek with Malcolm opening up the Word of God to me. I loved his British accent and his style of communication was very addicting. Malcolm's emphasis on our newness in Christ was refreshing. His teaching on the blood covenant remains the finest I have ever heard, and I still use his teachings on water baptism as mandatory listening for everyone that I baptize.

I really never had a mentor besides Harry, but through Malcolm's teaching, I fell in love with the Word of God. This man challenged me with statements like, "I never preach a passage of Scripture until I have read the entire book 40 times to make sure I get the context correct." Forty times, are you kidding me? Yet, I believe he was honest and even if there was a bit of exaggeration there, the challenge went deep into me. Do not just handle the Word of God like any other book. Read it. Digest it. Pray it. Live it.

In just about every tape series, Malcolm would exalt Christ, reverence the Word, explain who we are in Christ, and why it matters. I fell in love with Jesus through my teacher who I had never met. Years later, we would meet, and though our paths were not destined to walk in the same direction, his teaching provided a firm foundation for me to build a life upon. God is like that. Almost every major Bible character had real issues. Beginning with our father Adam through Abraham, the Patriarchs, David, Solomon, and on through all of the New Testament heroes, they have major flaws. Other than Jesus, there is no one that did not fall, sin, or fail in some major fashion. Yet, God redeemed them, used them, and their lives mattered! So does yours and mine.

What we teach, blog, post on social media, etc. remains for others to digest. What are we giving them? Malcolm gave me a love for the Word of God. May I learn how to speak life, lift up the name of Jesus, and leave a deposit behind me that changes someone for the glory of God. May I have such love for the Scripture that it flows out of me not only in the pulpit, but also in every day conversation and makes people hungry for the truth.

Mike

When we left Cameron and moved back to KC, I again worked for the remodeling firm. This time I was pushing papers instead of bugs, but still, it was not what I intended to spend my life doing. Almost as an afterthought I offered to assist my church with a little free bookkeeping service until they could hire someone fulltime. When I made this gesture, it triggered a series of events that I could not have imagined. It would be very easy here to go off on a tangent about being a servant and how many times serving opens doors, but I will restrain myself for just a bit.

The very next week my wife and I were meeting with all of the big boys at the church in the conference room and they were making me an incredible job offer. "How would you like to work harder than you ever dreamed of for half of what you are making now?" I heard them say. What a deal! Don't get an offer like that every day. While it would take some major cuts in lifestyle, we felt that this was the Lord's leading so we accepted. After selling our brand new car and buying a very old Rambler station wagon, moving out of our brand new duplex into an old, drafty farmhouse, and relocating to Shawnee, I began an eleven-year stint as the church administrator.

This church was very blessed to have as its treasurer a man named Mike. Mike was a CPA, who graduated from Harvard with his MBA and was a very successful commercial real estate banker. Mike forgot more about accounting and business principles than I ever knew. If anyone ever wanted to intimidate someone, Mike could. Mike never did. This man was gracious and treated me as an equal. In fact, he treated me, a twenty-five year old, wet behind the ears, holding an associate of arts degree, as a superior. Mike had the ability to make me feel like I knew what I was doing and that I was doing it well. Time has of course revealed reality, but Mike never looked down on me or treated me with contempt. He was a friend, a financial mentor, and a great role model for me.

As the years rolled along we went our separate ways, but we run into each other and have had lunch a few times. Mike remains the same. He treats me as if I was someone special. I have a sneaky suspicion that most folks feel that way when they are with Mike. I recently conducted a funeral for a mutual friend and there was Mike, the first person walking up to me explaining how wonderful I was and what a fabulous job I did. Mike is like that. I pray that I can be like him. Over the last twenty years or so, I have accumulated multiple advanced degrees, written books, and have a bit of experience. People tell me that I can be intimidating and whenever they do, I pray that as I interact with young men I can be like Mike. I want others to feel special and for our Lord to get any glory, just as Mike made me feel every time we met.

Dr. Jeffrey A. Klick

Tillie

This wonderful saint went home recently and her funeral
was the one I just mentioned in regards to Mike. I knew
this delightful lady for almost two decades. She always
carried candy around with her and gave it to all the
children, including us older ones. She also loved to wear
hats. Those that knew her were drawn to her smile and
almost singsong voice. Her joy was infectious. You
probably know someone like Tillie, yet she was unique to
me. Tillie had been divorced and suffered through twenty-
three major surgeries. I did not even know it was possible
to have so many parts removed or repaired!

Through all of her suffering, she maintained a
wonderful, joyous testimony. She rarely complained and as
I would visit her in the hospital, it would only take a minute
or two before she had flipped the conversation from her
illness to how I was doing. As she lay in intensive care with
tubes everywhere, I would explain that I had an ache or
pain somewhere and she would feel sorry for me. It usually
did not take long for conviction to settle in as I visited with
this saint.

I shared at her graduation ceremony (funeral in layman's
terms) that one thing I appreciated and wanted to imitate
was Tillie's lack of bitterness. If someone ever had the right
to whine and complain, Tillie had earned it. Yet she never
did in my presence. I am sure in her quiet moments she
failed, but I never heard it. Not only did she not become
bitter over her failing health, she did not allow that nasty
root to spring up even regarding her former spouse. In fact,
she would bring both her ex-husband and his new wife to

church and they even took vacations together. Now I am not going to say that this is normal or should be, but the fact that they could do such things revealed a strength of character that I had not witnessed before. I know many bitter people that spew out their troubles to everyone and anyone that will listen; Tillie was not named among them.

I learned from this dear lady that family is important, sharing the good things with others is so much better than always dumping out our troubles, and that every person could use a smile and a piece of candy. There are times to unburden ourselves on others, but there is never a good time to wallow in bitterness. Tillie made her choice years ago to accept whatever came and to choose joy and she lived this out in front of many others and me. May I do the same.

When my wife was explaining to one of our granddaughters that Tillie had died, this five year old asked a penetrating question. "Who is going to take her place?" Now, that is a question isn't it? While it is true that each of us are unique and no one can take our place, someone has to step up and fill the void left by this godly lady. Will it be me and you?

Arnie and Curtis

These two friends could not be more different if they had planned it. One is an out-going, loud, emotional, fiery Italian from New York. The other is a slow, soft-spoken Kansas boy, so mellow that one is tempted to take his pulse to see if he is alive. Yet, they are alike in many ways. Both have left their country for the Gospel and both are highly effective in their work. One is musical, one loves babies. One has grand visions to reach the masses, and the other prefers to bring food to lepers. Both challenge me to my core.

These two men and their families have left behind all that was home and made a new one. They would both rather, and most likely will, die in their new land. They have given all to the call of God in their lives and they absolutely love what they do for the Kingdom. Now that is a goal, isn't it? Both have had their struggles, yet they keep on walking with Jesus. Their lives shout of faithfulness, diligence, and finding the right place in God's Kingdom. They are very different in their gifts, yet the same in their passion. Both are walking out the good works that God has prepared for them:

> *For we are His workmanship, created in Christ Jesus for good works, which God prepared beforehand so that we would walk in them. Ephesians 2:10*

The principle I learn from my very different friends, is that God has the works already planned. God is the one who decides what we should do. God is the one that will assure we accomplish what He desires. Our role is to walk in obedience. It really does not matter what we do as long as we are doing what the Master wants. If we really are His workmanship, and He certainly does not make mistakes or poor quality products, we will end up in a good place. We are not saved by good works, but we have some to accomplish. Why else did God leave us here after salvation? In addition, if God, the Master, has works planned for us, who are we to attempt to place an ultimate value on them? What if God, knowing all that He knows, determines that my work is different from your work? Who is to say which one is more important? God is the only one that has sufficient information to make such a judgment call.

My responsibility is to abide in Christ, seek His will, and walk in obedience. God and God alone, is the one that hands out rewards, evaluates the eternal impact of those actions, and has the blueprint for my role in His kingdom. Why should I worry about or compare my life with others? If you think about it that really is just plain silly. Maybe God has not called you to leave all to serve Him in another country like my two friends; does that change the significance of your service for Him where you are? Of course not. God has work for each one of us according to His eternal plan. My two friends found theirs, how about you?

Barnabas

One of my favorite characters in the Scriptures is Barnabas. This guy takes Saul, the church persecutor under his wing when no one else would, defends a young disciple Mark from some harsh accusations, and is known as the *Son of Encouragement*. How could you not love a guy known as that? Being a pastor is sometimes a very lonely, discouraging life, and it has been the guys fulfilling the role of Barnabas that have often kept me going. What a source of strength and encouragement it is to have men that love you, care about how you are doing personally, support you, and pray for you. There is a danger when you begin to name people because someone will feel overlooked and left out so I will speak in general terms. You guys know who you are anyway and when you read this, you can figure out whom I am referring to now, can't you?

I have men that meet often just to pray for my family and me. Can you imagine how that makes me feel? These guys, all employed family men, take time out of their life to lift me up to the throne of Grace. I am truly humbled and deeply honored by their sacrifice. As one friend of mine likes to say, "You have to be careful what you say around these guys because they will do it." I feel like King David when he longed for a drink of water from a certain well. Three of his mighty men heard the request, made the trek, fought through the enemy, and brought back the drink. David appreciated the sacrifice and poured out the drink as an offering to his Lord because he knew he was unworthy. So do I.

These men have their problems and have not been perfect men, but since when did that become a prerequisite for love and service? There have been family issues, financial struggles, sin problems and just about everything that anyone else deals with daily, yet they continue to be Barnabas to me. I can call any one of these men and they will give me time, support, a listening ear, their opinion and prayer. While each is different in personality, all are men of God that I depend on for support. There was no way Moses could hold his arms up without Aaron and Hur, and there is no way I can be an effective pastor without my guys.

As I think about these men, I am challenged to be like them. Will I drop what I am doing for others that have a need? Will I pray for other people that are hurting and need support? Do people have to be careful around me with what they say or I might just do it? May I grow to this place. Every pastor needs strong, servant-oriented people that are holding up his arms, will you be one? Everyone can pray, serve, and be a support to those around them. I can attest to the fact that there is a dynamic that takes place when the pastor is being supported in prayer and when he is not. Prayer does change things; someday we will know how much.

I have given you just a glimpse into a few of the people that have greatly impacted me over the years. Some I have spent a lifetime with, and others just a short period, but each has a place in my heart. In eternity, I hope we have the opportunity to explore these relationships in greater detail. I pray that I can somehow communicate to these people and others the impact they have made in my life. I also hope that with whatever time I have left in life, I can be a friend and support to others so there is a great deal to talk about in eternity. If we have been living our lives selfishly up to this point, there is still time to change. Ask the Lord to bring conviction and then the grace to repent and change our way of life. We all want to live a life of influence in as many others as possible before we die, and our God delights in answering such prayers.

Dr. Jeffrey A. Klick

Questions to Consider:

1. Have I stopped and remembered the unheralded servants in my life? If they are still alive, should I thank them perhaps?

2. Am I influencing anyone for good in my network of people? If not, why not?

3. Is there someone that God wants me to influence for His Kingdom? Go for it this week!

Chapter Seven - Those Who Follow Us

Look behind you, someone is there.

Many that end up reading this book will be married and most will likely reproduce or adopt children. With the addition of children into our lives, a whole new dynamic of interpersonal relationships begin. Little humans begin to populate our homes and many times they look and act just like their parents. It seems that the problems, quirks, fears, and irritating habits that we have are passed along to our children, except they are compounded due to the expanding gene pool of our spouse.

Parents will operate their homes based on some sort of underlying philosophy of parenting whether it is known and planned, or simply happens by chance. Both are a parenting style, one simply works better than the other does. Failure to plan leads to planned failure and not knowing what you are attempting to accomplish will guarantee that you will not achieve it. In my book, *Generational Impact; A Vision for the Family,* I use a phrase "All parents train, some just have a plan," and it is true. In that book I develop a detailed vision for parenting so it will not be repeated here, but it is critical that parents spend some time thinking and praying about the direction for their home. The children you have are following you somewhere, in fact, everywhere.

If you are married and have children, then God brought you a spouse and gave you children, and it was not a cosmic accident. The sovereign Lord of the universe thought it best for you to be married and to reproduce (or adopt); doesn't it make some sense that perhaps He might have a plan? If Jesus is Lord of our lives, shouldn't that include our marriage and parenting style as well? Does God have a plan for your home and if so, shouldn't we be about the business of finding out what that plan entails?

The Bible is a family centric book from beginning to end. Adam and Eve were married, Jesus was born into a family, and the Bible ends with a huge wedding feast. God chose to reveal Himself as our Father and we are described as the Bride of Christ. We are adopted into a family and refer to each other as brothers and sisters in Christ. Family is everywhere in the Scripture and God does indeed have a plan for each one. Our job is to discover it and implement it to the best of our ability with the empowerment of the Holy Spirit. So, how will your marriage function? How will you raise your babies, toddlers, and teens? What kind of a grandparent will you become? These questions are worthy of thought, planning and prayer.

Each family is a unique mixing of personalities, visions, and dreams. Like fingerprints, no two families are the same and our God is creative enough to know the plans and purposes He has for each one. The Scripture teaches that each marriage is a picture of the mystery of Christ and His bride. Part of that plan as explained by Paul in this reference:

> *"Therefore a man shall leave his father and mother and hold fast to his wife, and the two shall become one flesh." This mystery is profound, and I am saying that it refers to Christ and the church. However, let each one of you love his wife as*

himself, and let the wife see that she respects her husband. Ephesians 5:31-33

What all of this means is beyond my understanding, but what I do know is that God came up with the idea of marriage and He values it greatly. Our marriages somehow present a supernatural picture and many are observing us. How we live in our marriages is important and this should be bathed in prayer and obedience. With Christian marriages falling apart as fast or faster than those that do not know the Lord, the Church has been failing to value this sacrament and the cost is enormous.

The natural outworking of most marriages is reproduction. A couple will either have children or seek them through adoption and this too is a God given desire. God is our Father and we want to be parents as well. Once we have our own children, then what? We are given a child to take care of for almost two decades and many of us are clueless as to what we are supposed to do. Oh, we know we should feed, shelter and clothe them, but then what? Parenting is an awesome responsibility and should not be entered into lightly or carelessly.

The Scriptures are full of directions for parents and we can gain great insight by reading and obeying. For example, consider the following verses:

And these words that I command you today shall be on your heart. You shall teach them diligently to your children, and shall talk of them when you sit in your house, and when you walk by the way, and

*when you lie down, and when you rise.
Deuteronomy 6:6-7*

*Fathers, do not provoke your children to anger, but
bring them up in the discipline and instruction of
the Lord. Ephesians 6:4*

*Hear, my son, your father's instruction, and forsake
not your mother's teaching, Proverbs 1:8*

Just from these four verses, there is enough direction to
begin to understand our duties as parents. We are to keep
the words of God in our hearts and to make sure we
diligently teach them to our children. We are to be careful
how we teach because we can provoke our children to
sinful behavior. We are to discipline them and challenge
them to listen to our instruction, and of course, the children
have the responsibility to learn and obey. How many of our
families would be radically changed if we simply attempted
to accomplish these few things?

Since God created the family and because He has a plan,
we must seek Him and discover what He desires for us to
accomplish as parents. Others certainly can help and
provide direction, but the responsibility rests with the
parents. Our current generation and the one following is in
crises, what will we do about it? If we will not take up the
challenge who will? If we will not invest in our children
and do whatever is necessary to lead them, who will? If we
do not know our plan, vision and what we would like to see
in our children, how will we know we are making
progress?

Parenting will lead us into many places we typically would rather not venture into. As parents, we will very quickly be faced with discipline issues, clothing choices, entertainment standards, relational strains, in-laws, and a host of potential conflict situations. There will be times of great stress, tears, and frustration. There will also be unbelievable joy, laughter, and pleasure. The journey can be enjoyable, and will be, if we follow the Maker's instructions. Sadly, many in our day are not enjoying marriage or their children, but rather choose to simply endure marriage or simply throw their children away, and it truly is a shame. God designed both to bring great joy and pleasure but our unwillingness to follow His instructions produces death and destruction.

Once we have conceived or adopted children, we have assumed a lifelong commitment. The truth is that we will be a parent until we die. Many times in my life I have looked for the PRG - Parental Resignation Department, yet failed to find it. My children will always be my children and my life will be constantly speaking into theirs. What is being said? What would our children say about *our* marriage or parenting methods right now? Fortunately, for us all, God is a God of mercy and new beginnings and He gives grace to the repentant! If we have failed, and we all fail, we can run to Him and find forgiveness, strength and the grace to continue on.

Knowing how messed up our world is, and the fact that many young people are leaving their parent's faith after moving out, we must seek God's direction while there is time. If our children are still at home, we can change the atmosphere of our home. Most young people that rebel will

Dr. Jeffrey A. Klick

state that hypocrisy in the home was the number one reason for their own faith rejection. This conclusion makes perfect sense if we think about it. If we proclaim that we are followers of an all-powerful, all-loving God, yet we demonstrate daily in our lives that He does not exist, what will our children eventually believe? Children will catch what we believe by our actions and not our words alone. Some self-evaluation time is typically needed to honestly consider the image of God that we are presenting in our home. Is it consistent with what we present when we are out in public, at church, or with other Christians? If not, we are on the road to assisting our children to reject what we teach them.

If our children are grown and already out of the home, we still have time to think about how we represented God to them. If we have failed, and again, we all fail, then we can and should ask for forgiveness and honestly attempt to rectify the specific failures with our children. We can also attempt to not repeat them with our other children or our grandchildren. And, we can share our failures as an example for others not to repeat! Everything, even our mistakes, can be redemptive in the hands of our redeeming God!

As parents, there are little eyes and ears around us constantly. What are they seeing and hearing? Our words, actions, inaction, and body language communicate volumes to these little sponges. What are they soaking up from our lives? Seeking God for patience, wisdom, faithfulness, and direction for those in our wake is very important. In fact, an entire generation hangs in the balance waiting for what we will do.

Questions to Consider:

1. Have I considered those that are following in my footsteps and what they are daily observing?

2. Will I seek to understand my Biblical role in marriage, parenting or being a godly single?

3. If someone followed me around all day recording my words and actions, what would the recording look like? What would I like it to look like? Are some changes in order?

Chapter Eight - Sweeping Back the Ocean with a Broom

Sooner or later we all take a stand, choose wisely.

In my opinion, the ocean is one of God's greatest creations. I love to stand on the beach and watch, feel, and listen to the magnificent roar of the waves. The sheer power of the majestic rolling of the water and the decibel level is breathtaking. Hour after hour, the waves come in, and sweep away whatever is in their path. Oh, we pretend that we can stand there and resist, perhaps jumping into a wave feeling somewhat powerful as we feel the ground sucked out from around our feet. But in our hearts, we know that if that wave were just a bit higher or stronger, we would be swept away like a ragdoll. Most of us have seen the damage caused by storms and an angry sea, and we marvel.

There are waves that sweep in upon each of us on a daily basis regardless of where we live. They may not be made of salt water, but they still suck the sand out from under our feet and attempt to knock us down and drag us away. I live in Kansas and the ocean is a thousand miles away, but that does not matter, the waves keep coming. Sometimes we feel like we are the only one attempting to stand against the wave, but still we must hold our ground. While sweeping back the ocean with a broom can lead to frustration, it is what we are called to do. God wants us to hold our ground no matter how fierce the storm. We are to keep on keeping on even if we feel we are not making any

Dr. Jeffrey A. Klick

progress. As long as the ground we stand upon is firmly based in Scripture, we must keep sweeping!

There are many such waves, but one foaming whitecap that we must resist is the one that demands that we conform to the norm. Peer pressure is well documented and if we are honest, we know it is not limited to school age children. There is pressure to conform at work, play, church, school, and just about anywhere two or more gather. Some pressure from our peers is helpful, like learning how to be kind, giving, and loving. Other types not so much, like jealousy, envy, self-centeredness, and off-color humor.

The only sure way I have found to resist being swept away is to anchor to an unmovable object, and the only sure foundation is Christ and living in obedience to His Word. As believers, we must look to His commands and attempt to walk them out daily. Jesus said that everything that can be shaken would be. I have experienced an earthquake or two and it is a strange sensation. The main problem in earthquakes, besides the destruction, is that whatever you grab on to moves. When we attempt to anchor our lives to a constantly shifting standard, we are living in an earthquake. There is only one foundation that does not shake, and that is Christ.

With the picture of waves and shaking structures in mind, let me venture into three arenas that might be a bit touchy. I would caution you first that if what I say is something that really bothers you, please check it out in the Scripture before reacting. I firmly believe that some of the struggles we see in the Church today are because we are looking at the wrong standard. We have replaced the Scripture with a shifting, shaking standard of popular opinion, or peer dependence. In the end, only what God has said will really matter and His Word is the final standard to be obeyed. With that caveat, let me venture into places where angels fear to go!

Modesty

There I said it, or wrote it. God said the following:

> ...*likewise also that women should adorn themselves in respectable apparel, with modesty and self-control, not with braided hair and gold or pearls or costly attire, but with what is proper for women who profess godliness—with good works.*
> *1 Timothy 2:9*

> *But sexual immorality and all impurity or covetousness must not even be named among you, as is proper among saints. Ephesians 5:3*

> *Now the works of the flesh are evident: sexual immorality, impurity, sensuality, Galatians 5:19*

There are many other passages that could be listed, but these are sufficient to make my point. Believers in the Lord Jesus Christ are to be noticeably different from those that do not know Him. How we think, speak, act, and even look, should be different. Visiting just about any gathering of people on a warm day will reveal (pun intended) what I mean. The lack of clothing displayed should shock us; however, most of us are not even concerned. The flaunting

Dr. Jeffrey A. Klick

of the female body has become so commonplace that to even bring it up raises shouts of "legalism," "bondage," "grace," and "who do you think you are?" "I am free in Christ." Granted, we are free in Him. However, that freedom is restricted in multiple ways.

In these three passages, freedom is clearly limited. Ladies are supposed to be modest in their clothing. Experts may argue over what this means, but ask just about any man, and it is pretty easy to understand what is modest and what is not. The apostle Paul told the people in Ephesus that these types of behavior should not even be named among you. The NIV translation uses the phrase, "not even a hint of," and I like that a bit better. This way of saying it brings to my mind, a fragrance, whiff of a smell. Do we have any immorality hanging around us? Do we smell of sensuality? Are we seductive in how we stand, dress or speak? How about our Facebook photos? These things ought not to be.

Christian weddings often seem virtually no different from non-Christian regarding clothing or the lack thereof. Sisters in the Lord are exposing themselves in the name of fashion. Cleavage, short skirts, skin tight clothes of all manner leave little to the imagination any longer. Athletic outfits of spandex and running outfits that are simply colored underwear are very common among the Church. Why? When did we move from covering up to exposing and uncovering ourselves? Why do we feel it is perfectly normal to reveal what should be reserved for the marriage bridal chamber? Bikini's, co-ed swimming, and all manner of exposure are common for the saved and unsaved. Why? Given the abundance of problems with pornography, lust, infidelity, and self-image, why are these topics of discussion avoided like the plague?

Part of the answer to these questions, I believe, is that we quit comparing our behavior to the Scriptures and began to look at Hollywood and society. This shifting standard of morality that is acceptable in the world around us has become the Church's standard. An honest evaluation of how the entertainment industry has changed over the years will reveal how far we have lowered the bar for decency. What used to be unnamed is now flaunted. What was once restricted because it was considered inappropriate is now acceptable. The same is true in the typical gathering of believers. When we stand looking into the mirror of the world instead of the Word of God, we will see a very different image that we should.

The Scripture states modesty, decency, and not even a hint or fleeting aroma of sensuality or seduction. The world is saturated with these things, and the Church seems indifferent regarding them. If someone dares to question or raise the issue, they are shouted down as a legalist or extreme. Just about anyone that questions the undressing of America is considered strange and out of touch.

For example, if someone says, "Why is it okay for godly women to expose their breasts either in swimming garb or wedding clothes," we are the strange ones? If we ask, "Should men walk around with their shirts off and wear skin-tight jeans?" we are out of line. If we question short skirts or shorts, and/or emblazoned lettering across a woman's chest or backside, we are thought lust crazed animals. Why does a woman put words like, "hot," "available," or "pink," on their chest and seat if it is not the goal for men to look there?

Most women know the power of their body and the influence it has on men. Looking "hot" is not due to the heat of the day but the enhancement and highlighting of the body. Yes, men have lust issues, and they need to control their thought life. But the question has to be asked as to the sister's responsibility regarding her temple of the Holy Spirit as well. Why do you want to draw men's attention to certain areas of your body? Why do you wear clothes that are tight if not to reveal what you look like? Motives need to be examined and the Scriptures need to be our standard, not a perverse culture. When we compare ourselves to the world system around us, perhaps we are doing well; however, when we look into the Word of God, we will change. The works of the flesh are evident, Paul states, and being sensual is clearly one of them.

I am not presenting a check list for modesty, but making an earnest appeal to consider our motives when we choose our clothing. If in doubt as to what a man would think about what you are wearing, ask one that you trust; you might just be surprised. Someone has to begin to resist the tidal pull of the ocean of immodesty; will it begin with you and me?

Fads

In my life, I have seen long hair on guys and short hair on women. Beatle boots, miniskirts and granny dresses, tie-dyed, pony and duck tails, streaked and no hair, mohawks and grow-overs, pointed and round shoes, piercing, tats, and just about everything else one can imagine. Fads come and go quicker than the weather changes in Kansas. Some are harmless and others can lead to real problems. There are music fads, worship fads, preaching fads, and architectural fads. We are surrounded with them. Popular gifts like the pet rock, and TV shows like Mork and Mindy come and go very quickly. My question in bringing them up is what should believers in the Lord Jesus Christ do with them?

Perhaps a deeper question might be asked - Is the Church supposed to be counter culture, a sub-culture or to change culture? If we are a sub grouping like farmers vs. city dwellers, or condo vs. home owners, then that is one thing, but if we are a counter culture group, that is something altogether different. Counter means someone that is not of, but in. The Scripture states the following:

> *If the world hates you, know that it has hated me before it hated you. If you were of the world, the world would love you as its own; but because you are not of the world, but I chose you out of the world, therefore the world hates you. John 15:18-19*

We, as believers in our Lord Jesus, are still in the world, but we are not to be of the same value system or hold to its definition of what is important. It has been stated (by my friend Malcolm among others) that the price tags are all messed up in our world and I would agree. What is important to the world system is not important to the Kingdom system. We pay spoiled athletes and entertainers millions of dollars yet the military and fire/police, who risk

Dr. Jeffrey A. Klick

their lives, are paid practically nothing. Those that devote
their lives to teaching children are paid sparingly, but if you
can sing or pretend (actor), you can be rich. Honesty and
charity are mocked while selfishness and the ability to tell
lies well are marveled at and encouraged. Okay, that is
mostly in politics, but still, the point is valid. The value
system of our ancestors has been replaced with something
else.

With that backdrop, why would we want to participate
in the passing fads of the world system around us? Why
would we want to embrace and promote those behaviors
that we should be opposed to? Why would we want to
encourage our children to adopt the practices of the system
that we are told will hate us? Why give those under our
care a taste for poison? If we look like, act like, think like,
dress like, laugh at the same humor, and participate in the
same things as the system that we are diametrically
opposed to, how is that being different? How will this
world hate us if we are simply a sub culture? Counter
culture is the way to go!

We should be a different group of folks. When off color
humor is used, we should not participate. When lying is
encouraged, we should stand for the truth. We should be
those that walk in moral purity, value what is honorable,
and promote what is righteous. When these issues clash
with the surrounding culture, and they certainly will, we
must stand firm on the side of what is scriptural. How else
will those that do not know Christ see a difference? If we
are exactly the same and there is no difference, we are in
danger of losing our saltiness. How we entertain ourselves
should be different. What we allow our children to embrace

ought to be different from those of the world system. Shouldn't it?

To repeat, I am not for making a long list of rules, but for examining our heart motives before the throne of God and checking to see why we do the things we do. Do we embrace a fad because we want to fit in and be accepted? Or to avoid potential ridicule from those that do not love Christ? Are we embracing something that is destined to perish or last for eternity? Excellent questions to consider in prayer.

Politics

Modesty, fads, and now politics? What, do you have some sort of twisted need to make people mad? Not really, but I have been around long enough now to have developed some rather strong opinions. The first president I voted for was Jimmy Carter. President Carter boldly proclaimed to be a born again believer, and so have many candidates since. Even the most non-religious ones typically end their speeches with, "God Bless America." I am not sure some of them really mean that however. Many of the presidents since Mr. Carter have made promises to reduce deficits, shrink government, and change this, that or the other. For the record, none of them have been successful in their claims. People who study such things state the government is huge, those dependent on it has grown almost to the point of destruction, and the political system continues on with endless debates and broken promises of change.

I am very grateful that I live in America and still have some say over who my leaders are. Many countries do not offer this opportunity. America is still a great place to live and while our freedoms are eroding, we still have some, and for this I am grateful. I vote, and strongly encourage others to vote and support their favorite candidates and positions. I even put out yard signs if I really believe in someone. Please participate and do not ever give up hoping that repentance will come to our nation.

However, my ultimate hope is not in Washington, Topeka, or whatever your local capital is. My hope is in a different Kingdom. I serve another King and my citizenship is in another Country! From the natural perspective, I have seen politicians lie, cheat, steal, and mislead all for the sake of re-election. Even men that I believe are Christian have compromised and not held to the standard of Scripture in the face of the media or political pressures. These godly people have disappointed me by their actions, but that is not the reason for this section of the book. Misplaced hope will lead to frustration and discouragement. I often state that, "In order to be disillusioned, one must first have an illusion", and it is certainly true in the political realm.

Looking to the political system to solve your spiritual issues will not work. Jesus did mention politics on one occasion. He said such radical things as, "pay your taxes" and "submit to those in authority," but do not be like them! I do not believe Jesus ever taught rebellion or commanded His followers to act in defiance of those in authority; He certainly did not model that as He allowed those in power to abuse and ultimately kill Him. Jesus preached a different Kingdom with an out-of-this world standard and understanding. When we attempt to mix the two kingdoms, we end up in a mess. The Dark Ages and early Roman Empire come to mind for example.

An understanding hit me one day during the time of the "Moral Majority" movement, which was a groundswell of Christian voters who were being motivated to become involved in the political debate. The thought I was struggling with was that every writer of the New Testament lived their life under a total despot and had none of the political freedoms we have, yet the Church grew and flourished. The Moral Majority was exerting some influence in the political realm, but would it last and make any real difference? The influence of Jesus, Peter, Paul, James and John has lasted 2,000 years, what has become of the Moral Majority in less than twenty years?

Today we have tea and coffee parties, and various groups that exert some measure of influence in the world of Washington, but for how long? Even if successful, these groups will soon pass away. I hate to be cynical about politics, but my hope is not in the political system. I have learned that God is not a member of either of the major parties, and neither is He part of the minor ones. My hope is in the Lord and His Kingdom. I await Jesus' return to right the wrongs and to establish His eternal rule. Jesus Christ will come again and set up His eternal Kingdom. He will reign as King of Kings and Lord of Lords, and of this Kingdom, there will be no end. Putting your hope in anything less than this is not wise and you are destined for disappointment.

So, please do vote, campaign, recruit, and help the candidates you support, but do not misplace your hope and lose your perspective. The eternal is the most important and the temporal will pass away quickly. We who follow Christ are citizens of another country and everything about us is different from those bound to this world. I pray that God will raise up godly men and women to political office and that our dear nation will return to its roots and values. However, I will not lose my faith if it does not. I love my birth country but I love my second birth country even more.

Resisting immodesty and sensuality, not giving into the ever changing world of fads, and refusing to place your eternal faith in temporal politics does feel like sweeping back the ocean with a broom. What is the alternative however? Caving in? Adapting? Compromising? I refuse! As long as I am in the air space that few venture into, let me address another somewhat controversial issue. Before reading on though, why not spend some time reflecting on what was shared in this chapter with the following questions.

Questions to Consider:

1. Am I just going with the flow of my culture or standing against it?

2. Have I given into peer pressure regardless of my age? Should I continue to do so?

3. Am I fearful regarding the future or full of faith? Why?

Chapter Nine - Did Paul Wear a Toga?

There is no deception like self-deception.

To those outside the law I became as one outside the law (not being outside the law of God but under the law of Christ) that I might win those outside the law. To the weak I became weak, that I might win the weak. I have become all things to all people, that by all means I might save some. I do it all for the sake of the gospel, that I may share with them in its blessings. 1 Corinthians 9:21-23

The Apostle Paul was a Roman and lived as a Pharisee until he met Christ. While the Pharisees often get a rightly deserved bad rap, they also were not all evil. These men kept the nation together during enemy occupation and helped to preserve the Law of God for centuries. They preached the Word of God and were required to memorize all of it. While some of them were clearly corrupt, there were others that were awaiting the Messiah and attempted to walk in the truth and light they had. Paul, while misguided before he met Jesus through his vision, was a devout purist that wanted to keep the synagogues holy and undefiled. Paul honestly thought he was serving God while cleansing out an infection in the gatherings.

After Paul met Jesus, he devoted himself to the Gospel with the same intensity he had as a Pharisee. Paul was a motivated man who desired to share the Good News of Jesus with anyone who would listen to him. His travels and writings changed the world for the Gospel. Paul at one

Dr. Jeffrey A. Klick

place said, "All I know is Jesus Christ and Him crucified," and this summed up his passion. The verse I began this chapter with is pointing to this passion of sharing the Gospel with the lost at any cost to Paul's pride or heritage.

Paul's passion was Christ and he was willing to lay down anything to get the message out. What is interesting to me, and thus why this chapter has the title it does, is how often the verses about Paul's passion for the lost are used as an excuse for just about any behavior. "I have become all things to all people," is often expressed to me to explain why someone chose to dress a certain way, dye their hair some weird color, get a tattoo, play a style of music, ride a motorcycle, sin, compromise, or walk in self-gratification. The driving motivation of Paul was to reach the lost. Is that the same motivation that is behind our decisions?

Heart motivations are interesting, and except for the Lord and the individual to a lesser degree, no one else knows what is really going on in there. There is nothing inherently wrong with most of what I said in the previous paragraph, other than sinning of course, but are we really doing what we do with the same passion to reach the lost as Paul was when he wrote those verses? Did Paul really put on a Toga when speaking to the Romans like so many in our day wear the garb of their group? From black leather to tattoos, from piercings to head banger hair, needing the latest jeans or running shoes, hard rock to country style, racecars to motorcycles, are we really doing these things in order to reach the groups for Christ? Did Paul change his outward appearance when addressing the Greek philosophers or Roman groups? Did he really travel with a ready switchable wardrobe and jewelry so he could relate to his audience? When Paul travelled over the world and landed in seaports and pagan countries, did he take on their look so he could relate to them? Or did he mean something else?

Most of the interaction I have had with people using this passage of Scripture has been shown to be more in the excuse realm and not so much in the "reach the lost at all personal cost" realm. In fact, the changes made were desirable and something the person clearly wanted and did not cause any inconvenience to them. Paul, on the other hand, limited his freedoms and restricted his behavior for the sake of the Gospel. He would have had to die to his personal desires and training to interact with some of the groups; he would not have desired to join or imitate them. Paul meant by these passages that he changed his approach to sharing the Gospel with these people, and it had nothing to do with outward appearances or personal tastes. Paul spoke freely to those under the Law using the Law, and to those without the Law he spoke just as freely about Christ. Paul's goal and sole motivation was to reach the lost and share with them the life changing power of the Gospel. Is that our motivation by our behavioral choices, or are we simply gratifying a desire we have and using this passage as a convenient excuse?

> Live as people who are free, not using your freedom
> as a cover-up for evil, but living as servants of God
> 1 Peter 2:16

Like Jesus, Paul preached a death-to-self Gospel and not one focused on self-fulfillment. Taking up our cross daily is

Dr. Jeffrey A. Klick

never intended to point us to self but to others. We certainly
are free to change how we look, follow some group's dress
and appearance standards, but using Paul's passion to reach
the lost for Christ should not be the text given as the
reason.

Are you saying that I am not free in Christ to do
whatever I want? Yes and no. We certainly are free in
Christ, but freedom needs to be defined. I am not free to sin
or infringe on another's freedom, and all my personal
decisions need to be filtered through Scripture. Consider
Paul's admonition in these passages to the Corinthians that
were taking liberties with the grace of God:

> *"All things are lawful for me," but not all things are
> helpful. "All things are lawful for me," but I will not
> be enslaved by anything. 1 Corinthians 6:12*

> *"All things are lawful," but not all things are
> helpful. "All things are lawful," but not all things
> build up. 1 Corinthians 10:23*

While we possess great liberty in Christ, we must
evaluate our choices and see what builds up and what
enslaves. When we enter a season of justifying our
freedoms, we should consider our motivation for what we
are demanding. Perhaps we should consider these verses as
well when we consider how free we are:

> *"For though I am free from all, I have made myself
> a servant to all, that I might win more of them."
> 1 Corinthians 9:19*

"Do nothing from selfish ambition or conceit, but in humility count others more significant than yourselves. Let each of you look not only to his own interests, but also to the interests of others."
Philippians 2:3-4

We have a responsibility to use our great freedom for the furtherance of the Kingdom of God, and not to satisfy our carnal desires. Each decision we make has an effect on many others. How we speak, what we wear, where we go, how we entertain ourselves, and how we treat each other has a ripple effect in the Kingdom. I am free in Christ to take up my cross daily and to die to myself so others may live unhindered by my freedoms! I will cover this a bit more in the next chapter so please keep reading.

We are given great latitude to express ourselves, but we are limited in our freedoms when our personal choices intersect with others. We must look out for each other and be aware of how our personal choices, which in themselves may be perfectly fine, affect others. Paul limited his freedoms and never demanded to have his own way. When we begin to demand that others must leave us alone and not limit us, boldly declaring our independence, we are on shaky ground.

The second greatest law of the Kingdom states that we are to love others, and by doing so, we show how much we love our God. Part of the process of how we love others is demonstrated by how much we are willing to lay down our freedoms for their sake. If my actions cause others grief or struggle, then by God's law, I am compelled to lay down my freedom for love's sake.

Dr. Jeffrey A. Klick

In Paul's day one of the key issues facing the Church were the Gentiles and how the Jews could possibly walk with them in fellowship. From dietary laws to dress codes, these two groups did not mix well. As the Gospel spread, more and more Gentiles came to know Christ and a crisis was at hand. In Acts 15, a council was called and the arguing went back and forth over what to do with these non-Jews coming to Christ. The Pharisees who had come to Christ wanted to compel the Gentiles to follow the Law. The newly founded Church of Jesus was on the verge of exploding into pieces over this dilemma. Finally, the Holy Spirit spoke and brought a much-needed solution to the problem. It makes for excellent study so check it out in Acts 15 to see what was decided and how the leaders came to agreement. For our purposes, it is sufficient to realize that it was settled and that the two groups, though very different, figured out how to walk together in love without losing their own identity.

As the decision from the council spread out over the Church at large, problems would of course arise as to the details. Again, Paul gives us some excellent principles to follow:

> *It is good not to eat meat or drink wine or do*
> *anything that causes your brother to stumble.*
> *Romans 14:21*

> *Therefore, if food makes my brother stumble, I will*
> *never eat meat, lest I make my brother stumble.*
> *1 Corinthians 8:13*

Meat sacrificed to idols, dietary laws, and whether to eat a ham sandwich all caused major issues in deciding how to walk out the decision from the council in Jerusalem. Paul lays out some very practical and clear instructions in these two verses. Think about what you are doing in relationship to your brother and how your actions affect him. If in doubt, don't do it. This is still a good principle to follow in our daily interaction with others in the Body of Christ. Meat is not that big of an issue today, but Paul did insert in that phrase, "or do anything," and that still applies to us in our day.

When I get dressed, invite someone over to my house, or whenever I am around others in the Kingdom, *their* welfare must be my primary concern. If it is not, then I am not walking in love. Love does not demand its own way, but love seeks the best for others and that includes everything down to how my freedoms impact my brothers and sisters. Now that is something to think about! I am perfectly free in Christ, free to die to myself, free to esteem everyone as better than myself, free to become all things to all men that I might be used of God to win some for Him.

Questions to Consider:

1. Am I justifying my fleshly desires with a spiritual covering?

2. Do I consider others valuable and adjust my freedoms for their sake, or am I walking in lawful freedoms that are unhealthy for me or others? Should I continue in them?

Chapter Ten - Relationships Reveal What We Believe

God I love You, but Your people often present a real challenge!

And he said to him, "You shall love the Lord your God with all your heart and with all your soul and with all your mind. This is the great and first commandment. And a second is like it: You shall love your neighbor as yourself. On these two commandments depend all the Law and the Prophets." Matthew 22:37-40

For the whole law is fulfilled in one word: "You shall love your neighbor as yourself."
Galatians 5:14

On several occasions Jesus was confronted by His foes and they attempted to trap Him with their questions about the law. Like always, Jesus hits it out of the park with His answer. Love God and love others are not what they expected, well, at least not the second part. The religious rulers would agree with loving God first, but then they would have moved into a bunch of other laws and never would have included loving others. Jesus made sure they did not miss the intent of all those other laws given to Moses. We do not live out our life by our self, but in community. Personal salvation is the most individually oriented activity ever experienced, yet once we bow before Jesus as Lord and Savior, we are never truly alone again!

Dr. Jeffrey A. Klick

We are part of a huge, worldwide family and our lives will interact forever.

While Jesus' words would have been shocking, Paul the converted Pharisee's words were unthinkable. Paul furthered Jesus' reply and shortened it into a single sentence that is almost beyond our understanding. The whole law is fulfilled by how we love our neighbors, how can this be? Not only Paul but also the other writers of the New Testament agree:

> *Above all, keep loving one another earnestly, since love covers a multitude of sins. 1 Peter 4:8*

> *If anyone says, "I love God," and hates his brother, he is a liar; for he who does not love his brother whom he has seen cannot love God whom he has not seen. 1 John 4:20*

The big three, Paul, Peter and John, all reflect Jesus' words about loving others to reflect our love of God. John the Beloved, the one that leaned on Jesus' breast at the Last Supper, affectionately known as the Apostle of Love, has by far the clearest words to share, and these were most likely written 50 years after Jesus ascended, so there was plenty of time for their real meaning to sink in:

> *By this it is evident who are the children of God, and who are the children of the devil: whoever does not practice righteousness is not of God, nor is the one who does not love his brother. 1 John 3:10*

We know that we have passed out of death into life, because we love the brothers. Whoever does not love abides in death. 1 John 3:14

Anyone who does not love does not know God, because God is love. 1 John 4:8

No one has ever seen God; if we love one another, God abides in us and his love is perfected in us. 1 John 4:12

Do you want to know who the children of God are and who the devil's children are; check out how they love one another. Do you say you love God but do not really love His other children? John the gentle apostle of love, clearly says you are a liar. Do you want to know if you passed out of death into life? Consider how you love others. John says, "Do not say you love God and yet walk in an unloving way towards others," it just will not fly with this apostle.

Fast forward to our day and consider how we are doing in light of these clear instructions. If we stood on any street corner and took a poll soliciting the opinions of those outside of the Church, how do you think *they* would view our love for one another? Is the Church known for its love or for something less than this? Sadly, ask most unbelievers and they will state the Church is known for being moneygrubbers or for fighting and dividing over just about everything. Love would not rank real high in any survey and this is a shame given the clarity of the Word of God on the topic.

Dr. Jeffrey A. Klick

"Love" is used over 500 times in the Scripture; in fact, the most famous chapter in all of the Bible deals with the topic. Just about anyone that can read knows at least a little of 1 Corinthians 13. Why is this command such a struggle for the people of God? Why do we have such a hard time loving others? If this really is all that important, and it is, why are we not better at it? We have clear instructions in the Scripture, we have the indwelling power of the Holy Spirit, and we have plaques all over our house, yet we fail in this arena. Why?

While there are many possible answers, and most would be overly simplistic, the bottom line has to include unbelief and disobedience. We simply do not believe what the Scripture teaches on the topic and we are unwilling to walk in daily obedience. Wow, that is a harsh statement Jeff! Perhaps, but I firmly believe it is mostly true, and probably a bit understated!

Consider how we actually walk out our Christianity in the relationships that are nearest to us - our family. As husbands and wives, do we really esteem each other as better than ourselves? Do we look out for our spouse's interests and have little concern for our own? Are we walking in a "take up your cross daily" lifestyle in our marriage and homes? As men, do we really love our wives as Christ loved the Church, dying to our self, washing her with the Word, as instructed in Ephesians 5? As wives, are you walking in quiet submission, willingly lining up under your husband, walking in the footsteps of Sarah? Need I really go on to make my point about our homes?

To the young people still living at home (or not), are you really obeying God's commandment to honor and respect your parents? Are we walking in all submission, humility, and laying down our rights for the sake of everyone else we know? Have we made it our ambition to be the servant of all? Sadly, most of us would have to agree that we are not doing what the Scriptures clearly teach.

Are we really honoring our bosses, teachers, police officers, public officials, and those in authority as commanded by the Scriptures? Are we watching our words and attitudes toward those that exercise a position of authority over us? I honestly think most of us have an obedience problem, not a lack of information issue.

How about in the Church? Can we allow others to disagree with us on the millions of personal issues that are not clearly revealed in Scripture? Can we refrain from judging one another over practices and decisions made that are not covered in the pages of our Book? To TV or not TV, computer or not computer, internet or not internet, eat certain foods or abstain, honor certain days or ignore them, use a certain translation or prefer another one, meet in schools or only homes, congregational vote or elder rule, hymn out or chorus out, need I go on? Our lists of requirements for fellowship and acceptance are long and many times exceed what is clearly written in Scripture.

So, are you saying that these differences do not matter and are unimportant? Not by any stretch of the imagination! I pastor a church that has a very clear, narrow focus of ministry that is defined by many issues that are not spelled out in the pages of the Bible. Every group will have underlying philosophies that help define their group. The love issue arises when we interact with those who do not hold to our personal views; that is when sparks tend to fly!

Dr. Jeffrey A. Klick

When we move into the realm of becoming exclusivists and thinking we hold the sum of all truth, is when we are in trouble. The reality is there are many issues in the Body of Christ that are not a matter of right and wrong, but right and left. These decisions represent personal choices that each church body makes to express their identity and ministry goals in response to the leading of Christ, and they should not be used to divide or attack one another.

These differences and lack of clarity in the Scripture always causes me to wonder why God put the Bible together the way He did. Please do not take this wrong, but I could have done a better job of giving specific instructions than the Scriptures do. If I had written the Scriptures, I would have included a chapter with specific details on how to conduct a church service, wedding and funeral, how to set up a board and budget, what ministries are allowed and which should not be, if buildings are allowed or only home fellowship meetings, and I certainly would have cleared up some of the difficult texts, like in Daniel and Revelation! God did not choose to do so, even though He certainly could have, so there must be another reason for His actions.

As I have pondered this thought, I think I understand at least one reason why He had the Bible written like it was. I believe God wanted there to be differences of opinion! Why would God do that? Is He mean or something? I do not think so. I believe the reason is so that we would learn how to love one another *in* our differences. It is relatively easy to love those with whom we agree, not so much with those who we do not. Even non-Christians love those that they agree with, but it is a supernatural demonstration of the reality of God when those who disagree walk together in love! God could have made sure that there was no room for controversy, yet He chose not to so there must be a reason for that choice. Love is a good reason.

God defines love in multiple ways including the laying down of our life for others, the sending of His Son paying the debt we owed, and He even made sure there was an entire chapter devoted to explaining what love is and is not in 1 Corinthians 13. Even a casual reading of this chapter will show that love is demonstrated in a relational fashion and is necessary because there are disagreements. "Bears all things, believes all things, hopes all things, endures all things," if that is not speaking about relationships, I do not know what else is! Love never ends and it never fails.

The world is waiting for the Church to actually take Jesus' words to heart and love one another. If the whole world will know we are His disciples by how we love one another, as Jesus clearly stated in John 13:35, we had better get on with the assignment! I am all for sending out missionaries to the ends of the earth, but Jesus said the world would know Him by how we are living our lives in community with other believers. What would happen to our Gospel presentations if we really were practicing what we preach in this arena?

There are many churches and groups that are attempting to bring unity to the Body of Christ, and these need to be commended. My call is for you and me, right where we live, to begin to walk in love with those around us. It is fine for me to applaud those other folks, the ones that I do not know for their efforts, it is perhaps more difficult to walk in love and unity in my home, workplace, and local

Dr. Jeffrey A. Klick

congregation. If all of us would begin to love those we know and to walk in obedience in our own world, change would take place. Slowly at first, but as it spread, the world would take notice, at least those in our world, and that is the power of the Gospel.

Questions to Consider:

1. Would those around me say I love God based on how I love others?

2. Do I treat others well and extend them grace, as I desire them to do for me?

3. How do I speak about those that I do not agree with?

Chapter Eleven - To Forgive is Divine

I want to forgive but it hurts too much.

Once we live on this earth for a few years we will encounter multiple opportunities to learn how to walk in forgiveness. People are human and because they are, mistakes, failures, unkind words, actions, and a host of other sins will occur. Unless you live completely by yourself on some deserted island, you will encounter those humans, and you will be hurt. In fact, you will hurt others. What you choose to do from that point on will have a major impact in your life!

Forgiveness of sins is one primary reason Jesus came to save the descendants of Adam. Another reason was so the children of God could learn to walk in forgiveness towards one another. We freely forgive because we are freely forgiven. This is especially true in our homes where the potential for unforgiveness is huge. Consider Jesus' answer and the example presented to His disciples after they asked Him to teach them how to pray.

> Give us this day our daily bread, and forgive us our debts, as we also have forgiven our debtors. And lead us not into temptation, but deliver us from evil. For if you forgive others their trespasses, your heavenly Father will also forgive you, but if you do not forgive others their trespasses, neither will your Father forgive your trespasses. *Matthew 6:11-15*

Dr. Jeffrey A. Klick

As Jesus explained to His disciples how to pray, these words must have been as shocking to them as they should be to us. "Forgive us our debts *as we* also have forgiven our debtors," and "If you forgive your heavenly Father will also forgive, but if you do not forgive others…neither will your Father forgive *your* trespasses." This is an amazing, often overlooked promise from the Lord Jesus Christ. How we forgive others has a direct relationship to how we are forgiven.

In Matthew 18:20-22, Peter was discussing how many times to forgive his brother and was feeling pretty generous when he suggested the unheard of amount of seven times. Jesus must have shaken him to the core when He explained that number needed to be greatly multiplied. In fact, in the rest of chapter 18, Jesus tells His shocked disciples a story about two men that were debtors. The first one owed a king an amount of money that was staggering and yet the king felt compassion and released the man from the debt. This recently released, forgiven man finds a man that owes him just a few coins and he begins to choke him and soon sends him off to jail, in spite of his pleas for mercy. The king is told what happened and severely disciplines this ungrateful wretch. While we may agree with the moral of the story, the punch line is just that, a punch. In verse 35 Jesus ties it all together with this sentence - *So also my heavenly Father will do to every one of you, if you do not forgive your brother from your heart."* Ouch. Jesus is the One that said it, and it is a promise.

In our daily interaction within our homes, conflict will arise. Feelings will be hurt, good intentions will be misunderstood and counted as something less than that, discipline will be misapplied, words will be stated more harshly than they should have been. In short, wounds and offenses are bound to happen. What we do with them will have a tremendous impact on the spirit of our home.

If we are the offending party, we must seek forgiveness from the one we hurt. As parents, it is a very healthy action to ask for forgiveness from our children if we have overstepped, overstated, or overreacted. The Scriptures state that fathers need to be careful not to provoke their children to anger (Ephesians 6:4) and we can do so by failing to ask for forgiveness from our children when we are in error. Pride is wrong regardless of our position and walking in humility is always the right response.

The same response of asking for forgiveness is true in husband/wife relationships, children to parents and child to child. Children will need to be trained to think and act this way, and a helpful method of getting this into the spirit of a home is for the parents to model it.

When this asking and receiving of forgiveness takes place, a home will navigate the difficult relational waters that naturally occur with people sharing the same space. When forgiveness is not taught or modeled, anger, resentment, and bitterness can take root. Hurts, wounds, and sins that are not confessed and cleansed by walking through forgiveness, fester and can turn into a relational mess. The Scripture states it this way:

> *See to it that no one fails to obtain the grace of God; that no "root of bitterness" springs up and causes trouble, and by it many become defile.*
> *Hebrews 12:15*

Dr. Jeffrey A. Klick

This verse states that we have a responsibility to make sure we do not allow this bitter root to take up residence in our homes or in us. If we fail here, this verse promises that trouble and defilement will follow. One sure way to avoid this root causing damage to our homes is to practice the giving and receiving of forgiveness quickly.

We did nothing to earn the forgiveness of our Lord Jesus Christ. We did not have to perform in a certain way, we did not have keep our noses clean for a set amount of time, or any other such condition that we sometimes place on others. We received forgiveness when we asked for it, and so should those that hurt us. Technically, we received forgiveness before we asked for it, even before we knew we were guilty and dead in our sins and trespasses. Therefore, we should forgive others quickly and that includes those under our roof. Jesus even forgave those that crucified Him (and they certainly did not ask for forgiveness) and presented a pattern to follow. We do not need to debate the point of timing regarding when to forgive; we simply need to give as we have received.

Put on then, as God's chosen ones, holy and beloved, compassionate hearts, kindness, humility, meekness, and patience, bearing with one another and, if one has a complaint against another, forgiving each other; as the Lord has forgiven you, so you also must forgive. Colossians 3:12-13

Relationship difficulties are common and will happen in every family. How will we deal with them? I would suggest we begin by rereading what Jesus told His disciples.

Forgiveness and Sin Issues

Outside of our family we will have contact with many others, and as I have stated previously, the potential for offenses, sin and forgiveness abound. The Scriptures reveal a clear way to handle the sin issue between His children.

> *If your brother sins against you, go and tell him his fault, between you and him alone. If he listens to you, you have gained your brother. But if he does not listen, take one or two others along with you, that every charge may be established by the evidence of two or three witnesses. If he refuses to listen to them, tell it to the church. And if he refuses to listen even to the church, let him be to you as a Gentile and a tax collector. Matthew 18:15-17*

The key word in this passage is sin. Sin is not being offended, overlooked, irritated, or any other lesser problem. These real issues, though not sin, have other options available on how to handle them and I will discuss them in just a minute. If we are sinned against, we are to go *directly* to the person that did the sinning first. The temptation here is to either avoid them or discuss the matter with everyone but the one who did the sinning. A great deal of harm, gossip, slander, and overall death to the Body of

Dr. Jeffrey A. Klick

Christ could be avoided if we walked in obedience to these verses.

It is human nature to want others to agree with us, support us, even sympathize with us, and it is not human nature to want to confront others in an uncomfortable conversation. However, we are told to go to the one that sinned against us first before we begin to talk to others. If we talk to the one that sinned against us and they listen, we have gained a brother or sister. If they refuse, then we take further steps. Many times we skip the first step and begin to tell everyone else about our pain. This is wrong and unleashes further sin in the Church.

What was written in the previous chapter about relationships is true, and how we walk through sin issues is important. These are sin issues, not personal taste or differences of opinion issues, but clearly revealed violations of God's Word. If someone lies about us, or steals from us, or violates us in a clearly sinful way, we begin this process of restoration. That is what this process entails, a desire to make everything right and restore fellowship. Our heart motives must be carefully examined to make sure we are not walking in punitive desires rather than having restoration as the goal.

If someone has sinned against us and after going to them they refuse to repent, *then* we take the next step of enlarging the number of people that know about the sin issue. If the person still refuses to take responsibility then it is moved to a still larger forum and then finally, the entire church is involved. This should be a rare process and walked out carefully under the guidance of the leadership of the local church! Again, the goal should be restorative not vengeful.

Offenses

Whenever two people spend much time together, the opportunity for rubbing each other in the wrong way multiplies. Everyone has a unique personality and sooner than later, something will happen in the relationship that is offensive. A harsh word, angry look, insensitive action, or personal choice will bug us. At that moment (and I am not referring to sin issues here) we have several options Scripturally.

> *Good sense makes one slow to anger, and it is his glory to overlook an offense. Proverbs 19:11*

We always have the choice to overlook the event and let it go. An honest evaluation of ourselves will reveal that we can be just as harsh, angry, and unkind, as the next person. Maybe the person was having a bad day or was simply not thinking. We do not have to react, but we can overlook.

> *Love bears all things, believes all things, hopes all things, endures all things. 1 Corinthians 13:7*

We have the option to quietly bear whatever offensive thing that was done because of our love for this person and in light of God's love for us. I believe this chapter also says something about love not being easily provoked or keeping

Dr. Jeffrey A. Klick

a record of wrongs suffered, but I will leave that to you to read from the plaque we all have somewhere in our homes!

> *We who are strong have an obligation to bear with the failings of the weak, and not to please ourselves. Let each of us please his neighbor for his good, to build him up. Romans 15:1-2*

We can look out for the other person and think of them, rather than how we are feeling at the moment of offense. We can bear with the failings of others and therefore practice the Golden Rule. Who is the strong one? Who are we to please? These two questions help us to walk in overlooking offenses and to practice forgiveness and mercy.

> *So whatever you wish that others would do to you, do also to them, for this is the Law and the Prophets. Matthew 7:12*

We all like to be given the benefit of the doubt when it comes to our own actions, and we can and should do so to others when it comes down to theirs.

Another option when we are offended is to realize that the person that wounded us probably did not realize they did so. We all have blind spots in our life and by nature these are unseen. Jesus said it in a humorous way if we visually grasp what was spoken:

> *Why do you see the speck that is in your brother's eye, but do not notice the log that is in your own*

eye? Or how can you say to your brother, 'Let me take the speck out of your eye,' when there is the log in your own eye? Matthew 7: 3-4

In my early days of following the Lord a comic team called Isaac Air Freight did a routine with this Scripture that was painfully hilarious. The "Logger Family" had these huge beams sticking out of their eyes and they were always breaking windows and furniture as they attempted to help others see their own faults, and it was funny to follow their experiences, well sort of. The painful realization of my own failures in this arena always seemed to spoil me from having too much fun at their expense.

Offenses will come and relationships will be tested. Love is our primary calling card to a lost and dying world; what do they read in our lives? Will we overlook offenses? Will we properly deal with sin issues? The instructions are clear; the only thing lacking is our obedience.

Many dear saints of God are paralyzed over events that happened to them decades ago. I am not dismissing the pain or heartache suffered, but it is time to move on into forgiveness. We can let go of the wounds of the past and embrace healing. We must learn to not let what happened to us in the past dictate what we will do or be in the future. God knows the pain and He understands the wounds. Jesus forgave the very ones that killed Him. Will we forgive the ones that hurt us? We have been forgiven a huge debt we could not pay; will we release those that have sinned against us? Maybe, just maybe, it is time to move on.

Dr. Jeffrey A. Klick

Questions to Consider:

1. What does the Golden Rule mean to me? Am I practicing it with everyone I meet?

2. Is there a root of bitterness in me, no matter how small? Should there be?

3. Will I release those in my past and forgive them? Should I?

Chapter Twelve - Servant Life

Cleaning toilets is extremely spiritual.

It must have been very ego building to walk with Jesus as one of His men. The twelve participated in or witnessed most of Jesus' miracles. When Jesus was feeding the two crowds consisting of thousands, the disciples were given the privilege of handing out the bread and fish. I do not know exactly how that would have taken place but I can imagine. Peter, with his big hands tightly holding to a small loaf of bread, began to break off chunks, perhaps a crumb at first as he started giving it out. As Peter broke off chunks of bread, the loaf never got any smaller. Weird. Soon, Peter began to give half loaves to those seated, and again, the loaf never got any smaller! On the other hand, perhaps there was a single loaf in the bottom of the basket. As it was given out, another took its place. Soon the basket had multiple loaves and no matter how many were given out, more appeared. We do not know how it happened, but the disciples were part of it and marveled!

These twelve followers of Jesus saw the dead raised, leprosy healed, blind eyes opened, the lame dancing, and multitudes of sick and demon possessed healed. In fact, at one point Jesus commissioned them, empowering them to do the same thing He was doing. You can read about it in Luke 10. Healings, supernatural provision, demons fleeing, these men experienced more than any tent revival preacher could ever hope to see in his meetings! I am sure pride and ego were a constant temptation. After all, Jesus did hand pick each one of them and by implication, did not pick the other guys. We are given some glimpses into the personal ego struggles that took place when we read about arguments concerning who is the greatest among them, and who would have the highest seat of honor in Jesus' Kingdom. Jesus, very aware of their struggles, cut through all of it with these instructions:

> But Jesus called them to him and said, "You know that the rulers of the Gentiles lord it over them, and their great ones exercise authority over them. It shall not be so among you. But whoever would be great among you must be your servant, and whoever would be first among you must be your slave, even as the Son of Man came not to be served but to serve, and to give his life as a ransom for many." Matthew 20:25-28

What had prompted these words was a mother asking Jesus that her two boys would be given a honored place in His Kingdom. As Jesus discussed this with her, the other ten became indignant, or we would say, jealous. Jesus gives them the key to greatness in His reply and it has nothing to do with social position, money, power, or whom you may know. It has everything to do with what we do and why.

Jesus called Himself a servant. Paul's frequent description of his position was a bondservant of the Lord Jesus Christ. So were the description Peter, James and Jude gave of themselves. Jesus came to serve and He says that we should have this same mindset.

And they came to Capernaum. And when he was in the house he asked them, "What were you discussing on the way?" But they kept silent, for on the way they had argued with one another about who was the greatest. And he sat down and called the twelve. And he said to them, "If anyone would be first, he must be last of all and servant of all." Mark 9:33-3

As the disciples were arguing about who was the greatest, I have to wonder what the expression was on Jesus' face. Was He smiling, thinking, "Come on guys, have you not picked up this truth yet?" Was He getting a bit perturbed, righteously of course, but angry about the pride and arrogance of the discussion? Was He toying with them trying to get them to see the foolishness of the discussion? After all, Jesus had just told them in the previous verses that He was going to die and they are fussing about which one of them is the greatest. We do not know what His face looked like, but we know what He said and did. After saying the above to them He brought a child in their midst and told them to become like one of these! We are not to become childish but child-like in our faith and obedience.

Now before the Feast of the Passover, when Jesus knew that his hour had come to depart out of this world to the Father, having loved his own who were in the world, he loved them to the end. During supper, when the devil had already put it into the heart of Judas Iscariot, Simon's son, to betray him Jesus, knowing that the Father had given all things

> *into his hands, and that he had come from God and*
> *was going back to God, John 13:1-3*

If you were reading these verses for the very first time, what would you expect to happen next? Jesus knew His time on planet earth was drawing to an end. Jesus had perfectly fulfilled His mission so far and He knew that the Father was giving all things into His hands. Jesus knew He came from God, was going back to God, and was in fact, God. At this point in the story we might expect a speech or parable of some sort from Jesus. Perhaps Jesus would explain what heaven was like, or how creation took place. Maybe He would draw back the curtain of mystery surround God, and since He came from Him and was going back to Him, He might give some juicy tidbit of information that no one else could possibly have know. What Jesus did was shocking.

> *...rose from supper. He laid aside his outer*
> *garments, and taking a towel, tied it around his*
> *waist. Then he poured water into a basin and began*
> *to wash the disciples' feet and to wipe them with the*
> *towel that was wrapped around him. John 13:4-5*

The Master, Lord of the universe, Creator, Teacher, and God Incarnate, washed His disciple's feet. This was slave work. This menial chore was reserved for the youngest, lowest in the pecking order, not for Jesus! Obviously none of them had offered to do the job of taking the lowest place, so Jesus did. Peter refused initially, then in typical fashion plunged headlong into the conversation - "Wash all of me,

Lord." This act of humility might have been the final straw to push Judas over the edge, for this was radical behavior on Jesus' part. Jesus explained to them that He was modeling for them how to live their lives. "You call me Lord and Teacher, and I am," He said. "I have done this to you, you should do this to each other." Thus the Savior provided a pattern for us all.

Okay, nice history lesson, but what does it have to do with us? Everything! If we want to be a follower of Christ, we must walk in His footsteps. The narrow path that leads to life is only wide enough for a single file journey. We walk in His steps, doing what He did, having the same attitude He had. Jesus was a servant and we are supposed to imitate Him. So, are we supposed to have foot washing services? Many have, but I don't think that was the only point of what Jesus did. Perhaps shoe shining services would be more in order in our day. The bottom line is that we are to learn how to serve everyone else in our life.

I said, "learn" because serving is not natural to most of us. If the truth were known, we would have the same discussion the disciples did if we were part of the twelve, because most everyone wants recognition and acknowledgement. Jesus is commanding us to do something that is not natural but is supernatural. Thus, we need the grace and the power of the Holy Spirit to choose against our nature. Learning to look beyond ourselves takes training and hard work. Most of us were not born with desirable traits like death-to-self, sharing, thinking more highly of others than our self, and a host of other Biblically commanded disciple traits! They are trained into us.

Dr. Jeffrey A. Klick

The family is an excellent place to begin the process of learning how to be a servant. Husbands can serve their wife and wives can serve their husbands Children can and should be trained to share, pitch in to help, and serve their siblings. Even toddlers can learn to carry out trashcans. Serving should be at the center of a godly home. What would our homes and churches look like if everyone actually took Jesus seriously regarding this topic? If each person was looking out for the interests of others and attempting to out-serve everyone else? The world would take notice.

Look around you with an eye to assist someone and you will discover an unlimited opportunity for ministry. Almost every day, each one of us will meet people that need help in some fashion. From a kind word, to opening a door, to allowing someone our parking place, to helping complete some task, opportunities abound. We simply have to look with a renewed sense of purpose. If you do not know where to start, then as soon as your feet hit the floor tomorrow, look around. Do clothes need picked up? How about the sink you wash your face in, does it need a cleaning? Do you know how to wash a dish, run a vacuum, empty trashcans? How about your spouse, anything they need assistance with today? Or your children? When we leave our homes, the opportunities expand exponentially! Everyone we meet or interact with provides an opportunity for service just waiting to happen. If we look, we will find.

Helping others does not take all that long and the rewards are eternal! Jesus said if we even give a cup of cold water in His name (Matthew 10:42) we will not lose our reward! How long does it take to give a cup of water to someone? How much time does it really cost us to let someone else go first in line or take the better parking spot? How about those that cut in front of us on the highway? Can we serve someone by letting them get ahead of us or does our competitive edge arise and we get upset? Expressing a kind word, opening a door, helping to pick up something dropped, offering an arm or a prayer, how long do these things really take? What were we going to do with those few moments we spent helping someone else anyway? Most of the time, the few seconds we invest in serving others is better spent than what we were going to do anyway.

As we begin to serve, amazing things happen. We often overcome myopia and start to notice others. The Holy Spirit will bring to our attention new and creative ways to help others as we yield to His leading. Needs are everywhere and we are the people that have the resources to help meet them.

As a pastor, it has struck me that some people join a church and instantly fit in. Others may go there for quite a while and never feel connected. Comments like, "No one reached out to me." "That place is so unloving." "There is nothing to do there," are often heard. Yet, the people that are involved do not feel that way at all. Why? Observation for the last 30 years reveals that those that give and serve make friends quicker and identify with the group, while those that wait to be invited often do not.

If you are lonely, reach out to other lonely people. He who shows himself friendly will have friends. It seems that there are always a few people that tend to make up an "in-group." Everyone wishes that they would be included, and often stand around by themselves longing to be noticed by these two or three people. My advice is to forget the perceived in-group and begin to reach out to the others longing to be in that exclusive mix. Start your own group with everyone who is outside of the cool group and you will have plenty of relationships! We tend to limit this thinking to the awkward moments in our school days, but they still apply today, we are just a bit older now.

Look for some place to serve and it will not be long until you find others that like doing the same thing. I have never met a servant complaining about boredom and lack of friends. Maybe the church is not really the problem.

Living for others will bring you peace and joy, while being selfish and self-absorbed, will leave you with you. Not too many people enjoy being around a self-centered person, yet they are drawn to a servant. If you want to be great in Jesus' Kingdom, you must follow His commands. Learn from Him, be a servant and watch your life explode with purpose.

Questions to Consider:

1. Would I rather serve or be served?

2. What would those that know me the best say about question one?

3. What would our marriages and homes look like if we really did begin to attempt to out-serve one another each day? Will we try and see?

Chapter Thirteen - Dare to Pursue Our Dream

With God there is no fear of anything that is not God.

Each of us is created in the image of God and He has prepared works for us to accomplish before we leave this planet. Ephesians 2:10 is clear about this. So, what do we dream about in our walk with God? What is in our heart of hearts that perhaps no one else even knows about it? What lingers in our minds and motivates us? What would we do if we could, and time, money, and abilities were no object? Is this just a waste of time or does God place this desire in us to challenge us to step out further in Him? Are we limiting what God could do with us by our fears, doubts, and lack of faith in Him?

As I read the pages of Scripture, I marvel at how ordinary the Biblical heroes are, other than Jesus, who was of course God and perfect. Abraham? He was so fearful he told those in power that his beautiful wife was his sister so they would not hurt him. Isaac did the same thing. Jacob, with a name that means "deceiver," he really did not have too much of a chance anyway. Moses? If I remember correctly, he had a bad temper, killed a man, and would have been an interesting leader to attempt to serve under. David? Solomon? Even everyone's favorite Daniel; Where was he again when his three friends were not bowing down? While we really do not know, I doubt if he was on vacation somewhere. A reading through the heroes of the faith in Hebrews 11 is more like a listing of losers than a litany of character examples to follow.

Dr. Jeffrey A. Klick

The point is that there was only one perfect Man, and that was Jesus. The rest of the characters in the Scripture were just like you and I. Yet, our hearts soar when we see God using normal, sinful, humans to accomplish supernatural purposes. Man is made in the image of God and is empowered with will, desire, abilities, reason, gifts, and imagination. Jesus made some pretty incredible statements that are either true or they are false.

> *He said to them, "Because of your little faith. For truly, I say to you, if you have faith like a grain of mustard seed, you will say to this mountain, 'Move from here to there,' and it will move, and nothing will be impossible for you." Matthew 17:20*

> *And Jesus answered them, "Truly, I say to you, if you have faith and do not doubt, you will not only do what has been done to the fig tree, but even if you say to this mountain, 'Be taken up and thrown into the sea,' it will happen. Matthew 21:21*

> *If you ask me anything in my name, I will do it. John 14:14*

There are many books written to explain these passages and what they *really* mean and I have no desire to argue with the authors. My point is that these verses mean something, and what I see is great potential to do incredible things for God! Regardless of our age, gender, race or spiritual maturity, we can move mountains with faith and nothing is impossible for us when we are walking with our God.

Our deepest desires, when aligned with God's will, have all the power necessary to be accomplished. Our God holds the universe together by a word; is He limited by anything that we could come up with in our brains? If we are abiding in Him and He is us, we can ask what we will and it will be accomplished (John 15:7). While I certainly do not know all that this means, I understand enough to know that Jesus in me equals great things for His Kingdom. As I learn to yield to His will, listen to His still small voice, and walk in obedience to His revealed commands in the Scripture, there is nothing that cannot be completed.

So, what is your dream? What is in the deepest part of your heart that only you and God know about? Is it too big for the Creator and Sustainer of the universe to handle? Perhaps that desire is there because God wants to use you to further His work in this world. What a concept! It would be unthinkable except we have a Bible full of God doing so with the most unlikely characters. A shepherd boy slays a giant. A fearful Gideon is turned into an army router with a handful of men with torches. The Patriarchs are really a bunch of jealous half brothers that sell their youngest sibling into slavery, yet God builds a nation from them. The Apostles were ordinary men that often squabbled about being important. Which of the heroes didn't have issues in their character? Yet, the story of the Scripture is God using imperfect people to accomplish His perfect will. Can He use you and me?

What has God put into your heart? Write a book? The book you are reading was written by a guy that hated school, yet now has multiple advanced degrees. Lead multitudes to Christ? Begin with those under your own roof, reach out at work and your neighborhood, and see what God Almighty can do. Sing, serve, teach, give, it really does not matter, if we are abiding in Him, desiring that His will is accomplished over our own, we can and will do great things for Him. He is the one that ultimately decides what is great or not anyway! Go ahead, dream, abide, and take a step. You never know where you will end up if you just start serving those around you. Dream big because we have a big God.

As we age, we begin to realize that many of the dreams and goals we had when younger needed to be tempered and rechanneled. As youth gives way to experience, we gain a different perspective of what is important. I still play sports, but the edge is not what it was. Some would say, "He has lost a step," and in my case, several, but what is gone of youthful agility is replaced by experiential wisdom. Our outlook changes as we age and sometimes so do our goals, dreams and visions. Certainly, our value system should grow and mature as well as we reevaluate what success is and what it really means.

As we grow in our walk with God, our perspectives change. As the decades roll by, we see God's hand in our lives in ways we missed when we were living through it. Time often brings clarity. We tend to long for the eternal, having spent so much time saturated with the temporal. Laying up treasure in heaven, because we know we are closer now, takes on new meaning. How we spend our time and resources matters more now than when we were children. Time for the human is a limited, fleeting commodity. So what are we doing with what we have left? That is an important consideration, and where dreaming comes in!

We have works to accomplish and God has promised that we would. Remember the passage that this book is based upon? We have desires that He has placed in our souls and we long to do them. The question arises as to how. While I am sure it is different for each of us, some things are common to all of us. God desires to have a personal relationship with each of us. What a marvelous sentence! This same God has a will and we are included in that will. God has works for each of His children to accomplish and these are important to Him. The dreams and desires in our heart, as we abide in Him, are tied to the above sentences!

The Holy Spirit in each of us stimulates us to good deeds and prods us along the path of God's will. We have desires that are given by God and He will see to it that we fulfill our purpose. After all, He began a good work in us, He will complete it. Paul the apostle said we were God's workmanship and God does not make junk.

How do we begin to follow this dream or desire in your heart? We all know that "You cannot steer a parked car". I do not have God's email address, nor have I ever heard His voice audibly. Wish I had. However, if we are born again believers, we have the Holy Spirit right inside the deepest part of us. The Spirit leads through the Scripture, through impressions, and through circumstances. For me the way I have ended up in God's will is to begin the journey away from the curb! If something is in my heart to do, I begin to do it trusting that the Lord will give further clarity. God can

Dr. Jeffrey A. Klick

stop me, correct me, prompt me, open and close doors as to His will. I trust Him to lead, guide, and provide for what He wants accomplished through me.

Well, isn't that a bit presumptuous, Jeff? Consider these verses as my reply:

> *And they went through the region of Phrygia and Galatia, having been forbidden by the Holy Spirit to speak the word in Asia. And when they had come up to Mysia, they attempted to go into Bithynia, but the Spirit of Jesus did not allow them. Acts 6:6-7*

Paul was driving his car down the road and wanted to go into Asia, okay, probably he was on foot, but he wanted to go somewhere and the Holy Spirit clearly said, "No." The group then attempted to go into another city and God did not allow them. How this was done is not given for us to know, but the fact that it happened is clear. God can direct our driving, or walking, or what is in our hearts as He wishes, if we are listening to Him in prayer and seeking His will daily. Paul was out and about, willing to go anywhere to share the Good News, and the Holy Spirit directed as He wished. If Paul had stayed in Antioch, or wherever he was before the journey, the opportunity for the Holy Spirit's direction would have been lost. See?

For me, trial and error (with a great deal of prayer) works in finding God's will. As a godly dream arises in my heart, I begin pull away from the curb and drive in the general direction trusting that the Lord will make it clear to me what He wants. I am not demanding my will, but desperately seeking His. God has a purpose for my life and yours. Part of our job while we are living is to seek it out and begin to fulfill it! What is your dream? Strap on your seatbelt and start the car and drive!

Questions to Consider

1. Has God given me a dream? What would it take for me to step out in faith to begin it?

2. Am I attempting to limit God using me by my past failures? Should I?

3. Am I abiding in Him, spending quality time with Him, pouring out my deepest desires to Him? If not, why not?

Chapter Fourteen - Don't Give In or Up

God does not make junk, including me or you.

Thank you for allowing me to share with you some of what the Lord has been showing me over the years. God is good, and His ways are perfect. Each of us is dearly loved by our Heavenly Father and He has a plan for us! God has decided that He would use us to further His Kingdom work, and that is simply amazing.

We are God's workmanship and we were created to do good works that He has prepared for us. The journey to completion is not usually a straight line, but a curved road. There are many unexpected twists and turns in life, but these often end up being the most exciting times as we begin to view them from God's perspective.

> *Therefore, since we are surrounded by so great a cloud of witnesses, let us also lay aside every weight, and sin which clings so closely, and let us run with endurance the race that is set before us, looking to Jesus, the founder and perfecter of our faith, who for the joy that was set before him endured the cross, despising the shame, and is seated at the right hand of the throne of God. Hebrews 12:1-2*

Some people read this passage in Hebrews and think of a bunch of ancient dead people looking over the edge of heaven and watching them. Some have the unspoken thought that these saints are waiting for the runners to fall down so they can snicker or yell at them. "Hey loser, get up and keep going". Or perhaps they are saying, "Look at Klick down there stumbling yet again, come on man, get up and run straight." I prefer to think of a bunch of people looking out of windows as I run down the highway of holiness yelling out encouragement. "Don't quit, you are almost home". "Oh, he tripped, come on get up, we love you, we're with you, we support you." The cloud of witnesses went before me and their lives offer me hope and encouragement. Just knowing there are many ordinary people like me who made it helps me to lay aside the weight and run on with endurance. How you view God will impact how you walk with Him. Perhaps better stated, how you view God viewing you will impact how you walk with Him.

My God is for me. My God loves me. Through Him I can live a life that matters. My view of life is filtered through some basic understandings that give perspective to how I live my daily life regardless of what may happen. In addition to the ones I shared in the previous chapters, these provide strength and hope daily:

✓ God is either sovereign or He is not. If He is sovereign then what do I have to worry about? God is sovereign.

✓ God's Word is either true or it is not. If God's Word is true, then all will be well. God's Word is true.

✓ Jesus is the Son of God. He lived a perfect life and paid the price for my sin on the Cross, and because of that sacrifice I am now in Him. By being in Him, I am now a new creation, have a new purpose and vision for life, and will spend eternity with Jesus and all other believers. I am now a child of the King and dearly loved by my Father; what can man do to me that ultimately matters?

✓ I am invited to come to the Lord as often as I want. I am promised that I will receive grace and mercy in my time of need. The Sovereign Lord invites me to abide in Him, rest in Him, live in Him and be loved by Him. In addition to all of that, I have been given the Holy Spirit to live right inside of me. It simply does not get any better than this!

When I lose sight of any of these basic understandings I tend to drift and become discouraged. When I cling tightly to them, joy and perspective enter back into my heart. I am a masterpiece in progress and so are you if you are in Christ. God does not make junk and He will complete what He began.

From one work in process to another - rejoice!

My other books - available online at Amazon or via my personal website - www.jeffklick.com

What Others Are Saying:

"There is a lot of good discussion material in this book."

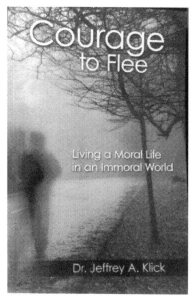

"Wonderful gems will be found in this book." "That one statement provided enough discussion between my daughter and me to justify purchasing this book." "I encourage families with young adults or children nearing adulthood to purchase *Courage to Flee*, read it, and then read it again with your older children." "*Courage to Flee* will give parents the encouragement they need to stay the course in an increasingly sensual world." **The Old Schoolhouse Magazine**

"*Courage to Flee*" by Dr. Jeff Klick is a much-needed book in today's culture where lust and impurity are common-place. The book provides a strong biblical warning to those approaching the slippery slope of impurity, as well as great hope and practical counsel to those who have slid down its banks and are now entangled in the mud and quicksand of sin. This book should be in the hands of every pastor, as well as every man and woman who needs to know the biblical solution to freedom and purity."—Mike Cleveland, Pastor of Preaching and Vision, Ohio Valley Church and Founder and President of **Setting Captives Free Ministry**

"It is an astounding work." Michael Aprile - **The Utmost-Way Magazine**

"I want to thank you again for writing such an important book. What a labor of love. May God use it to help thousands! I can highly recommend it!" **Books on the Path**

"Whether you are single, dating, courting, engaged, married, or parenting, *Courage to Flee* should be a book in your library." **The Courtship Connection**

"When you shared real life illustrations, it was powerful and impacting" "Outstanding book" "Thanks for already making an impact and perhaps saving a brother from a stumble or a fall!" **Glenn Miller- Miller Management Systems**

"Pastor Jeff Klick, author of a new book, "*Courage to Flee*," provides some helpful wisdom and hope to those who are in the spiritual battle of their lives." - **Generations Radio**

" I highly recommend this book and would recommend that you buy a case at a time. Give them away to others, buy a copy for your pastoral staff, give them to a youth pastor...it's just that good!" - Fletch - **The Mango Times**

Dr. Jeffrey A. Klick

"When I got to the end of the book where you begin speaking about the Church...I was saying Amen, Amen and Amen." **Debbie, mother of 4**

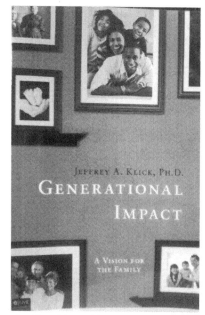

"Recently we finished reading your new book – and wish we'd had it when we started this journey as parents 6 years ago!" **The Burts**

"It is AWESOME! I have read and re-read the *Generational Impact* book and find so much wisdom and help in it. I love it!!!" **Tori, Stay-at-Home Mom and Piano Teacher**

"I have almost all of it underlined in yellow!" - **Tricia, Homeschool Mom of Three**

"Two thumbs up on your book. Very edifying...." **Peter Lindstrom, Pastor**

"Thanks for the new book! I read through it last night and liked the job you did handling a broad array of topics. I especially appreciated your wisdom in the last three chapters. My prayer is that many will read it and be blessed. Thank you for your continued ministry to the family!"- **J. Mark Fox, Pastor Antioch Community Church**

"It is a joy to read a resource by an author that is simply a pastor. He has not become a rock star in a denomination, he has not written any NY Times best sellers (though I wish this book was one!), he just goes about shepherding the flock that God has entrusted to him. Dr. Klick offers a complete theology from years of pastoral (and parenting) experiences. There is a great movement in the church today for the family to take back the impetus of the spiritual, physical, and emotional training of children. Add to that ever growing list of resources this one by Dr. Jeffrey A. Klick. It is one that you will read once, hand off to another, and then wish you had back so you could read it again only to realize that you are glad you handed it off to someone else! In other words, purchase a couple copies so you can give some away while keeping your own marked up copy in your library." **Christian Book Notes**

"*Generational Impact* gets into the nitty-gritty of many practical ways of passing the baton of the Gospel on to the next generation. This thorough, yet non-condemning, work is encouraging. It helps us approach the discipleship of our families from a biblical, contemporary and realistic perspective. I was personally delighted by *Generational Impact*, and immediately after completing this book I ordered one copy for every family in Vancouver Household of Faith." - **Eric Burd, Household of Faith**

"I thought you did a good job with the book, communicating important truths in a concise and readable way. I enjoyed reading it. May it find wide readership!" **Jonny White, Dean, Ekklesia Theological Seminary**

"I have read the "Generational Impact" book and really appreciate it. It is a wonderful resource not only for vision for a biblical family but practical ways to implement the teaching as well. I am grateful for pastors who are planting these biblical seeds with families. Should the Lord tarry, it will be seeds of revival and influence, we pray, in the generations to come." **Mark, Men's group leader in Minnesota**

Dr. Jeffrey A. Klick

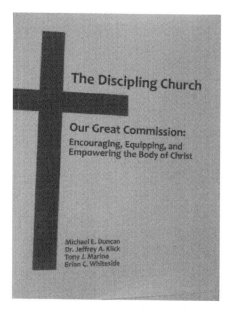

The Discipling Church

Our Great Commission:
Encouraging, Equipping, and
Empowering the Body of Christ

Michael E. Duncan
Dr. Jeffrey A. Klick
Tony J. Marino
Brian C. Whiteside

The Discipling Church offers a compelling case for why the Church in the West must increase Her efforts to make disciples. The book offers practical tools that will equip your church to both evaluate your congregation and also begin to make advancements in the mission of disciple-making.

Dr. J.R. Miller, Professor and Author in San Diego, CA
www.MoreThanCake.org

The Discipling Church is exactly what Christians should expect from a book on Discipleship. This is a powerful work meant to provide today's pastors and church leaders with a fresh reminder of the biblical methodology of discipling new believers in a contemporary post-modern, post-Christian culture.

Captain Roy Butler
US Army Chaplain

The Discipling Church is a complete, well-written study of the history and biblical foundation of Discipleship. I would recommend this book to anyone who seriously desires to understand and be involved in Discipleship. Also included in the study is an analysis of how the average local church is functioning in the area of Discipleship today and easy-to-use Discipleship Study Curriculum. This material may be used effectively as an individual or group study. Be prepared to be convicted about your personal walk with the Lord as you work your way through *The Discipling Church*.

John Hobson
Director of Missions, Mt Baker Baptist Association

The Discipling Church is an unveiled look at the true mission of Christ's body. We are to make disciples, period. So many today are at ease in Zion, lounging on padded pews, enjoying the blessings of Christ's labor, and searching only for a life of comfortable happiness. This book is a clarion call for believers to stop "going" to church, and start "being" the church. From an intricate biblical foundation, a consistent Christian worldview, and without diluting the gospel requirements of the disciple, *The Discipling Church* is an explication of the Great Commission of Jesus Christ, which asks all believers…Who are you discipling…and who is discipling you?

Jason Velotta
Pastor and Author of *Reclaiming Victory: Living in the Gospel*

If you would like to order and of my books in bulk quantities at a reduced rate or need to get in touch with me please visit **www.jeffklick.com** for contact information - May God richly bless you as you follow Him.

Dr. Jeffrey A. Klick

Helpful Websites:

http://www.christiandiscipleshipministries.com - Discipleship on steroids, check it out for resources.

http://www.christiandiscipleshipministries.com/onlinetv - Live as well as many podcasts of discipleship teaching.

http://www.aliveinchristradio.com - 24 Hour radio station on which I serve as part of a pastor's panel.

http://www.hofcc.org - Great network of churches.

http://www.c4fic.org - Resources for the family-oriented church pastor.

http://foundationrestoration.org - Resources for marriages

http://www.thehomeschoolchannel.tv - Resources for home educators.

http://www.michellehollomon.com - Christian life coach and counselor, also hosts a weekly radio show.

http://www.michael-duncan.net - Friend, co-laborer, excellent author and wordsmith.

http://www.ambassadorsforchristradio.com - Friends in Panama and radio show hosts.

http://www.morethancake.org - Friend, teacher, one creative dude.

Made in the USA
Charleston, SC
13 November 2012